IDAHO FISHING GUIDE

Hook, Line & Sinker

Pete Zimowsky
Illustrations by Patrick Davis

Contents

Alpine Trout 2	Bluegills 39
Brookies 5	Catfish 42
Browns 8	Crappie 45
Cutthroats 11	Perch 48
The Hunt for Goldens, and Grayling, Too ... 14	Walleye 51
Ice Fishing 18	Sturgeon 54
Reservoir Trout 21	Fly Fishing for Steelhead 57
Float Tubes 24	Using Plugs for Steelhead 60
Stream Fishing for Trout 27	Northerns 63
Trolling for Trout, Coho and Kokanee ... 30	Mackinaw 66
Wild About Whitefish 33	Catch-and-Release 69
Bass 36	About the Author and Illustrator ... 72

Acknowledgments

My first fly fishing experience in Idaho came about three decades ago when I took my first cast with a Potts hair fly for cutthroat trout in Crow Creek in the Caribou National Forest of southeast Idaho.
Two passionate fly anglers, my father-in-law, Andy Michaelson, and his father-in-law, Harry Nuckols, took me fishing for cutts and baptized me in a life-long sport.
They're gone now, but every time I cast a fly I think of them and thank them for passing on the tradition.
I've passed on the tradition to my kids. - *Pete Zimowsky.*

Two signs hung in his shop, hair cuts $1.50 and Gone Fishing.
He would have loved to fish Idaho. Pass me a worm, Pop. -*Patrick Davis.*

PORTLAND

© 1995 by Pete Zimowsky
All Rights Reserved. No part of this book may be reproduced without the written consent of the publisher, except in the case of brief excerpts in critical reviews and articles.
Illustrations by Patrick Davis • Book and Cover Design by Kathy Johnson
Published by Frank Amato Publications, Inc., P.O. Box 82112, Portland, Oregon 97282, 503•653•8108
Printed in Hong Kong • 1 3 5 7 9 10 8 6 4 2
ISBN: 1-57188-013-5, Softbound; 1-57188-014-3, Hardbound

Alpine Trout

Sometimes you learn more about fishing by just sitting on a rock and watching the lake. A trout taught me that lesson at Idaho's Bloomington Lake, an alpine lake deep in the Wasatch Mountain Range.

Some of the best fishing in Idaho is casting a line at an alpine lake. Idaho has about 2,000 high-mountain lakes that require anywhere from a mile to 10-mile hike. They may contain rainbow, cutthroat and brook trout, and California goldens or grayling. That's what makes fishing Idaho's high-mountain lakes fun—backpacking to a lake and finding out what kind of fish live in it. Alpine lakes let you combine hiking, mountain biking or backpacking with fishing.

But in a rush to fish a beautiful lake, surrounded by lush green fir trees and sheer granite cliffs, most of us go off half-cocked. The natural inclination is to cast as far out in the lake as possible. Most likely, you won't get any takers. In a lot of lakes, the middle is often barren. Why should fish hang out where there's an empty cupboard? When you get to a lake, sit down and take a rest. You'll probably need one anyway after the hike in. Watch the lake. Scan the shorelines. Then you'll see them. Trout rising for bugs just a few feet from shore. Sometimes, only inches from the bank.

After getting skunked at Bloomington Lake, I sat down and gazed around the lake wondering how I could be such a miserable fisherman. Suddenly, I heard it. "Gulp, splat." "Gulp, splat." A big, old mossy cutthroat was gulping bugs about three inches from a log. It was only about 10 feet from the bank. Each time it grabbed a bug, it would dive back underneath the log where it was safe. I crawled along the bank as quietly as possible, just as if I was fishing a small mountain stream and didn't want to spook the fish. I slithered on my stomach across a big flat rock and got into position. While lying down I flipped a small Hare's Ear Nymph right next to the log, almost right in the ripples left by the trout.

Bamm! The cutthroat was on and skipping across the water like a PT boat. That trout taught me a lesson I will never forget. In most mountain lakes, the grub is near shore and that's where the trout will be. The thing about fishing Idaho's mountain lakes is that every one of them is a surprise. It's a new adventure in hiking and fishing.

No matter what fish you find, go prepared. One thing you can't do is carry a full tackle box into one of these lakes. You want to go light. When I'm using a fly rod, I usually carry one small fly box with an assortment of small nymph and shrimp patterns like the Hare's Ear, Black Ant, and olive or gray shrimp patterns. The Prince Nymph is another good bet along with grasshopper patterns and some caddis patterns.

It's difficult to fish with a fly rod because most lakes have brushy banks and there's not much room for casting. The spinning rod is the best bet. If you will be spin fishing, take a small plastic pocket fishing box with nothing more than a few Mepps, Rooster Tail or Panther Martin spinners and several fly-and-bubble combinations. But remember one thing, in a high mountain lake, don't try to cast way out in the middle. The fish might be right under your nose, next to the bank.

What To Use

The Rooster Tail is a spinner that can be cast out and retrieved easily in a mountain lake. Retrieve it slowly, working it close to the shoreline. The best colors are yellow, black or yellow coachdog (yellow with black spots).

The Panther Martin is a killer in alpine lakes. Fish it the same way as other spinners. The best colors are the original, which is a silver blade with a yellow body with orange spots, or the Black Zebra with a black blade and a brown body with yellow spots. The Mepps spinner is another easy lure to use. Any of the lures with a silver, gold or black blade will catch fish. The Black Fury is especially deadly for alpine lake trout.

The fly-and-bubble combination is a great trick that allows the spin fisherman to fly fish. Normally you can't cast a fly with a spinning rod. Get a small, clear plastic bubble and attach it to your spinning line. About 18 inches from the bubble, tie on a fly, such as a Hare's Ear Nymph, small black or olive Woolly Worm or other green or brown nymphs. Cast the line out and let it sit for a few seconds. This allows the fly to sink. Then reel in about 3 feet, very slowly. This makes the fly seem as if it is swimming to the surface. Trout love it. If you don't get anything, let it sit again and then reel in another 3 feet, repeating the process until you get a fish.

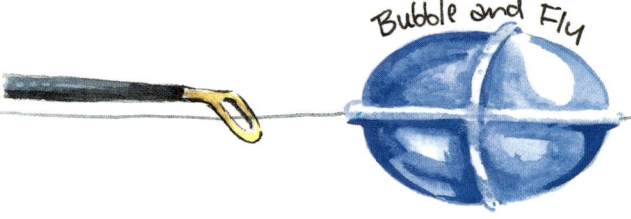

Where To Go

Idaho is blessed with 2,000 high-mountain lakes, every one of them fun to fish. Some of the best I've found for beginners to try are:

1. Boulder Lake: This 113-acre lake in the shadow of Jughandle Mountain is an easy day trip from McCall or a 2-hour drive from Boise. Take the Farm to Market Road east from Highway 55, just south of McCall. A few miles down the road you'll come to the Boulder Creek Road. Drive up the road to the trailhead at Boulder Reservoir. Boulder Lake is one mile from the trailhead.

2. Blue Lake: Here is another easy hike in the West Mountains, about 7 miles southwest of Cascade and 1 1/2 hours from Boise. Drive north on Highway 55 to the Clear Creek Inn and turn west on the road that goes to Cabarton. Just after crossing the North Fork of the Payette River, take the Snowbank Mountain Road to the Blue Lake trailhead. The hike to the lake is about one mile.

3. Trinity Lakes: The Trinity Lakes area is several hours from Boise. It is reached by driving I-84 to Mountain Home and taking the Sun Valley exit. Follow Highway 20 to the cutoff for Anderson Ranch Dam and follow the road on the west side of the reservoir to Fall Creek. Reached from the Fall Creek Road, the lakes sit on a mountain spine between the South and Middle Forks of the Boise River. You can drive right up to some of the lakes, including Trinity, and Big Roaring River. There are more than a dozen other lakes in which to hike.

4. Ruffneck Lakes: Once you've acquired your hiking legs, try something a little more difficult. Ruffneck Lakes in the Seafoam area, northwest of Stanley, provide a little more challenge (5-mile hikes and further). But the views and the fishing are worth it. It's about a 3-hour drive from Boise. Take Highway 21 northeast to Lowman and continue toward Stanley. Once you hit the Capehorn area, look for the turnoff north to the Seafoam area. There are several trailheads located along the road.

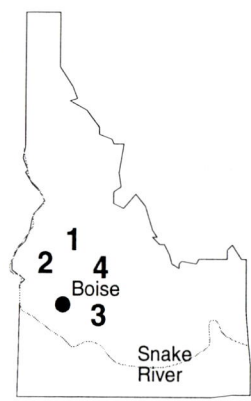

Brookies

Little rings rippled across the beaver pond in the mountains of eastern Idaho and instantly grew into large circles. "Golly, there are fish jumping in that pond," I yelled to the kids, as we drove by on the dusty, rock-strewn road in the Snowdrift Mountains. We were headed from Georgetown across the mountains to Diamond Creek, one of the blue-ribbon cutthroat trout streams in the area.

Needless to say, we didn't make it. I jammed on the brakes of my old four-wheel-drive and skidded to a stop. A dust cloud engulfed the whole car. Everyone started choking. The abrupt stop almost threw the kids and the dog into the front seat with me.

"Get out of the car. We're gonna try to catch whatever's in that pond," I told the kids. "String up your poles, but wait for me," I said. "We've got to sneak over there or all those fish are going to scatter." We must have looked pretty stupid, crouching down and crawling through the mud and willows to the edge of the pond.

"Somebody get the dog. If she goes for a swim, the fish will scatter." Luckily the dog felt more at home rolling around in the mud and didn't want any part of the gin-clear beaver pond water.

What had me going crazy was that the pond was no bigger than a backyard swimming pool. How the heck could there be any fish in something that small? The stream going out of the pond was small, too. How the heck did trout get into something this high in the mountains, and this far from the nearest big stream? The rippling circles continued to bubble across the pond in the middle of lodgepole pine and fir trees. It was a feeding frenzy. I don't know what the heck the fish were feeding on, but I don't think it would even matter.

"OK," I whispered to my son James. "Just flip the fly over the bushes and into the water. You don't have to cast very far."

He whipped back on the fly rod and immediately got the Renegade fly hung up on a tree limb in back of him. "Hold it. Everyone stay put," I whispered, crawling over to the branch and unhooking the fly. "Try it again, nice and easy," I said. This time James hit the mark and put the fly right over the bush and into the beaver pond. It didn't take a second for a swirl around the fly and his fly rod to start bucking.

"I've got him, Dad," James yelled. The fish danced across the water wiggling all over the place. I knew it was a brookie. Nothing jumps, twists and flies out of the water like a brook trout. No matter how small they are, they go nuts at the end of a line. After a few minutes of dancing around in muck up to our knees—we were in shorts—James got the fish in. Well, almost.

The fish was tangled around a mess of willows and wrapped around a stump. I was on my knees in cold mountain water with my hand reaching down, up to my elbow, trying to untangle the fish. I grabbed it and pulled it out of the water. It was a 13-inch brightly colored brook trout. It was one of the most beautiful fish I've ever seen. There's a certain magic about catching brookies. They're so wild it usually leads up to something like getting tangled in lily pads, around stumps or under a canoe.

You never know where you're going to catch brookies. They

can be in alpine lakes all over Idaho. You'll find them at the headwaters of a lot of streams. I've fished for them in the headwaters of the cutthroat streams in eastern Idaho and also in central Idaho in the Wood River and up Trail Creek outside of Sun Valley. I've found them in the high lakes around McCall and also at Bull Trout Lake near Stanley. They're in lakes in the Selkirk, White Cloud, and Sawtooth Mountains and Bighorn Crags. They're practically everywhere.

The fun thing about brookies is that they like to bite, most lakes have too many of them, and they fight like crazy. If you want to teach a kid how to fly fish, then do it in a brookie lake. Brookies also like small spoons and spinners, if you're a spin fisherman. And guess what? If you're a bait fisherman, all you need is a bobber and a worm.

If it sounds like I'm excited about brookies, you're right. Have you ever sat around the campfire at an alpine lake, frying up a pan of brookies for dinner? Well, just do it and you'll learn why brookies are good fighting and good tasting.

Yup, the colorful brookie is one of my favorite fish.

What To Use

Flies: If they're biting, it doesn't matter what fly you use. I've caught brookies on Renegades, Gray Hackle Peacocks, small black Woolly Worms, small black Woolly Buggers, small black ant patterns, and shrimp patterns. Try anything.

Spinners: Any black and yellow Panther Martins, Mepps, or Rooster Tails work well. Orange and yellow, and black and yellow are good color choices, too.

Bait: Use a bobber on your line. About 12 to 18 inches below the bobber—depending on the depth of the lake or fish—tie on a No. 12 hook. Put a split shot between the hook and the bobber, if necessary. For bait, use small pieces of earthworm, not nightcrawler. A nightcrawler is too big. You can also use grasshoppers or crickets.

Where To Go

You can find brookies almost anywhere. It seems game wardens back in the old days shipped brookies from back East by train and then hauled them up in the mountains by pack string. The fish are from back East, hence the full name, Eastern Brook Trout. After the fish arrived by train they were taken to high lakes by mules and horses. The fish were put in water in big metal milk jugs that were strapped to the sides of pack animals.

If you go exploring and try a lake, small stream or beaver pond, you may find brookies. If you do, you'll have loads of fun and plenty of fish for the camp frying pan.

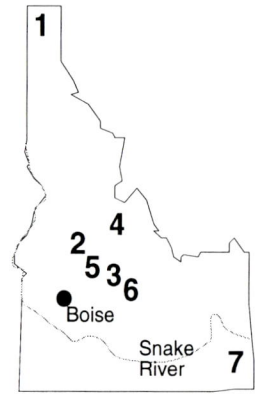

Here are a few places to go exploring: high lakes in the Selkirk Mountains in northern Idaho (1), around McCall (2), near Stanley (3) and over in the Bighorn Crags (4). I've even caught brookies at the headwaters of the South Fork of the Payette River in the Sawtooths (5). You'll also find brookies in some of the streams north and northeast of Ketchum (6) and in the ponds and streams in the Caribou National Forest of southeast Idaho (7).

Browns

A full, yellowish moon creeps over the high-desert, lava rock horizon. It almost looks like a space ship and sets an eerie tone for the evening fishing trip.

It's getting so dark, you can't even see the width of the Little Wood River south of Carey. Everything you memorized during the day is a complete blur. You can still hear the rushing waters, and you're hoping you don't step in a hole over your waders as you sneak into position to get off a good cast with your fly rod.

Soon your eyes adjust to the darkness and the moon is now totally up. It's like a beacon and you can see the light of the moon glistening off the silvery riffles. It also lights up the surrounding sagebrush and lava rock landscape, creating a mysterious atmosphere, one where you can't help looking over your shoulder.

Fishing for brown trout by moonlight is kinda creepy. As you creep along, step by step in your waders, the whole feeling is creepy. But hey, if you're going to catch big brown trout you've got to do it at night, and by the light of the moon is best. We're talking big browns here, the kind that don't mess around during the daytime.

Browns are nocturnal. Did you ever wonder why so many are caught at dawn or dusk, especially during the winter when the light is so much more faint? These browns don't want anything small. They're looking for a hardy meal. That's why when it comes to fly casting for big browns at night, most anglers use the Deer-Hair Mouse.

Fly casting at night is another thing. You're lucky if you don't hang up your fly rod in the brush or get that prized Deer Hair Mouse stuck on a log. Deer-hair flies don't come cheap at the

fly shop. Even if you're a fly tier, they're not something you tie up very easily.

Anyway, the Little Wood River, deer-hair flies and the light of the moon. What a combination for trouble, big trouble like in the way

of big brown trout. Fighting a fish in daylight is hard enough. What about trying to get one in the dark? Stalking brown trout by the light of the moon is an experience no one will ever forget.

Flip that Deer-Hair Mouse up against the opposite bank, as if the mouse just fell into the stream and is trying to swim to the other side. Strip in your line and make the artificial mouse dart across the stream. Any second now wait for a brawny brown to come soaring from the depths and take the mouse.

When that happens, look out. It'll be you and a monster fish fighting it out in the dark. Most likely the fish will win but that's the way it is when stalking browns by moonlight. If you do catch one of these big browns, turn it loose. We need to keep our brown trout populations strong. Anyway, a big brown is too good to only be caught once.

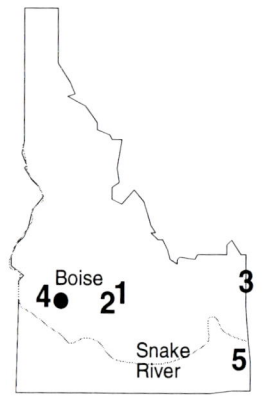

What To Use

Flies: Any version of the deer-hair mouse will do. The best fly rod is a 7, 8 or 9 weight fly rod, something a little bigger than for small stream trout. Use floating line with a short leader, about seven feet long. Make it 12-pound-test line.

Where To Go

1. Little Wood River: This well-known brown trout stream is located along U.S. 93-26 from Shoshone to Carey. In addition to good numbers of brown trout, the stream also has wild rainbows. Some browns have been known to go 6 pounds or more. The Little Wood River has special regulations on certain sections, so check them out before fishing.

2. Silver Creek: The section near Priest Campground is known to have large brown trout. The creek in this area is reached by driving U.S. 20 between the junction with Highway 75 and Carey. Check for special fly fishing regulations on sections of Silver Creek.

3. South Fork of the Snake River: This is one of the best-known brown trout streams in Idaho. You can fish or float several sections of the river from Palisades Dam downstream. The river is reached by driving U.S. 26 out of Idaho Falls.

4. Boise River: The Boise River through downtown Boise can be a brown trout fishing paradise for the angler willing to learn the hot spots. The urban river has produced its share of browns 5 pounds and over. It is easily accessible from town along the Greenbelt.

5. Stump Creek and Crow Creek: These two streams, which flow from eastern Idaho into Wyoming have good populations of brown trout, which come up from the Salt River in Wyoming. The easiest way to reach Crow Creek and Stump Creek is to drive northeast from Montpelier, Idaho to Afton, Wyoming, on U.S. 89 and backtrack back into Idaho from Afton.

Deer-hair mouse

Cutthroats

The cutthroats were killing the grasshopper fly. With each cast in the Middle Fork of the Salmon River, a cutthroat trout would come up and hit the fly pattern that I call the Sloppy Hopper. I try to tie the famous Joe's Hopper, but it always comes out a little too sloppy for that name.

But the cutts of the wilderness river didn't care. All I had to do was cast in front of a rock while our raft floated by and a fish would zoom up from the depths and nail it. I could do no wrong, I thought. I did do something wrong. I didn't bring enough grasshopper fly patterns and three-quarters of the way down the 100-mile river I was out of good flies. The good fishing ended. I couldn't get the fish to hit any other flies.

That's a mistake you don't want to make while floating Idaho's wilderness rivers like the Middle Fork of the Salmon, or the Selway.

You'll probably run out of gear before you know it. Cutthroats don't only take grasshopper flies. They like Rooster Tail spinners, Mepps spinners and Panther Martins. If you hang a few of them up on rocks or snag them on the bottom of the river while you're going through a set of rapids, too bad. You're out of luck. I once lost a $100 graphite fly rod in a set of rapids below Indian Creek on the Middle Fork. Trying to talk other boaters into lending their fishing rods while the cutts were hitting was futile.

Planning for a fishing trip on one of Idaho's wilderness rivers doesn't have to be that difficult. Just make sure you have the right gear and enough of it. There are no K-Marts on the banks of the Middle Fork of the Salmon River.

Float trips and trout fishing go hand in hand. The Middle Fork of the Salmon River offers some of the best fly fishing or spin fishing for cutthroat trout. It is definitely one of the best places to learn how to fly fish, too. Since the river is catch-and-release fishing, the cutts are plentiful. It doesn't matter if you make a bad cast or not. Somehow you usually hook into a cutthroat.

It hasn't always been like that. When rafting took off on the Middle Fork decades ago, you could catch and keep the cutthroats. They made pretty fine meals while camping on the river. But soon cutthroat populations started taking a dive. When catch-and-release regulations went into effect the fish came back. The Middle Fork is one of the best cutthroat streams in the United States. You can bet a Sloppy Hopper on that.

OK, so what does it take to float a wilderness river and be successful at hooking fish? Let's talk about it.

What To Use

If you're a spin fisherman, the answer is simple: Take along plenty of spinners, swivels and small spoons. You might take along an extra spool of line, extra rod and extra reel. You can snag up on a brush and have the whole fishing rod ripped out of your hands while the current sweeps your raft downstream. If your boat flips while you're fishing, you can also lose a whole mess of gear.

As far as spinners, if you only take Rooster Tails, Mepps and Panther Martins in a variety of models, you'll be OK. Don't get big ones, they must be comfortable to cast. You'll probably want to use 6 to 8 pound test line on your spinning reel. Some small silver, brass or red and white spoons will work too.

Any angler should take a pair of pliers along. Since it's catch and release, you'll want to clamp down the barb on your hook. You can only have one hook on your spinners and lures. Needless to say, no bait is allowed.

If you're a fly fisherman, grasshopper patterns are a must. Joe's Hopper or Deer or Elk Hair Hoppers are great. Don't forget other patterns, like the Renegade, Elk Hair Caddis, Royal Wulff, a variety of Humpies, and the Stayner Ducktail. Once on the Middle Fork, the cutts quit hitting everything. They didn't want hoppers or any caddis flies. It was perplexing. I tied on a Stayner Ducktail, cast out and let it sink about 6 inches below the surface before retrieving. Bamm! That was the fly for the rest of the trip. The Stayner Ducktail is a popular fly pattern tied in all the shops across southern Idaho.

Fly fishermen might take along a vise and some tying material. While in camp, you'll have plenty of time to tie a few much-needed flies.

Take along plenty of leader material with your supply of flies. It might not be bad to take a floating and sinking line, and extra rod and reel. No telling what can happen. You might hit a wave and fall on your favorite fly rod. The rest of the fishing trip would be history.

Where To Go

1. Middle Fork of the Salmon: If you want to fish this stream, you've either got to apply for and get a permit or go with an outfitter. Going with an outfitter is best if you've never floated the wilderness river. You'll learn a lot.

You can also be flown into a backcountry airport along the river and set up housekeeping with your backpacking equipment. The backcountry pilot will come back in a few days to pick you up. Check with wilderness fly-in services in Boise, Salmon, McCall and Cascade. You can also backpack your way into the Middle Fork country by taking the trail

in from Boundary Creek, Big Creek or several drainages on the Challis side of the river. There are also some dude ranches and lodges to stay at along the river. Check with the Idaho Outfitters and Guides Association booklet for details.

2. Selway River: Here's another river you have to get a permit to float, and it's not easy. If you get a permit, you'd better know what you're doing. This river is no piece of cake. You can go with an outfitter. The river is located in north-central Idaho near the Montana border. Another way in is to backpack.

3. South Fork of the Snake: This river is also cutthroat heaven. It is accessible from the road in Swan Valley near the Idaho/Wyoming border. You can also float it and drift boats are very popular on this river. Outfitters are also available for this river.

The Hunt for Goldens, and Grayling, Too

I've never caught a golden trout. Come to think about it, I've never caught a grayling. Idaho has both of them. I've just never been able to track them down. I've hiked to a lot of high-mountain lakes but never hit a lake with either one of these exotic species.

I call them exotic because they're not just your normal everyday fish. You've got to do a lot of research, then hike 7 to 15 miles to get to one of Idaho's remote alpine lakes that have golden trout or Arctic grayling. Grayling and goldens are not native to Idaho. They were stocked in high-mountain lakes decades ago. They took in some lakes and not in others. There's even a lake in the Bighorn Crags named Golden Trout Lake, but it doesn't have any goldens in it. They died out and were never restocked in the lake. Idaho Fish and Game plans to restock mountain lakes with grayling and goldens, but getting the eggs from other states is difficult because of the high demand.

Anyway, stalking goldens and grayling can be a lifetime passion. I know a few anglers who have been hiking to mountain lakes for 30 years and have never caught either species. If you're looking for grayling, you may want to search alpine lakes from 8,000 to 9,600 feet in elevation. They may be 15 miles from the nearest road. They may be in the Bighorn Crags, Lemhi Mountains, or in the Buffalo Hump area. Goldens, on the other hand, are a little more widespread. They may be found in places like the Sawtooths, White Clouds, Selway Crags or Copper Basin.

A lot of Idaho's 2,000 or so alpine lakes were stocked with different kinds of trout in the late '40s, when Idaho Fish and Game wanted to create some new fishing opportunities for the thousands of GIs coming back from World War II.

Alpine lakes are stocked with rainbow, golden, brown, cutthroat and brook trout and grayling. Some of the lakes were stocked long before that in the age of the milk can and mule fish-stocking operations.

Nowadays high lakes are stocked by plane or helicopter. Today they can stock a whole mountain lake with a gallon-size plastic bag containing hundreds and hundreds of fish. Of course, the fish are only an inch or so long.

Fish and Game publicized high lakes fishing as late as the mid-'70s when you could still get a small booklet put out by the department called, "Mountain Lakes of Idaho." The book was incredible. It listed mountain lakes throughout the state and told what kind of fish were stocked in each.

Soon afterwards, the booklet went out of print and was never reprinted. The reason, Fish and Game believes that fishing high lakes should be an experience of self-discovery. Each mountain lake is something new for each fisherman. Like I said before, some anglers make fishing alpine lakes a lifetime passion.

Don't expect to catch any whoppers when you get to one of these alpine jewels. You're just going to enjoy the experience of catching an exotic fish. Idaho's record grayling caught in 1992 was 2 pounds, 7 ounces. Most likely some of the grayling you'll catch in high lakes will be only 5 to 9 inches long and only weigh a few ounces. Golden trout are a little bigger. The record golden for Idaho was taken in 1958 and weighed 5 pounds, 2 ounces.

I'm not going to give you a blow-by-blow description on how to get to lakes with grayling and goldens. That would be a terrible

Adams

Mosquito

Ant

Renegade

injustice for all Idaho anglers. If you want to find them, it's up to you. I'll help you get started. So go out and stalk some goldens or grayling, if you're hooked on trying to hook an exotic fish.

What To Use

Both goldens and grayling have been caught on everything from salmon eggs to flies. Spinners work, too. The best gear to pack along on a trip to a remote lake with grayling and goldens

is a variety of flies and spinners. I hate to carry in bait because if you've ever spilled a jar of salmon eggs in your backpack, well, need I say more. And the thought of having nightcrawlers loose in your backpack alongside your bagels and cream cheese, ugh. So, let's stick with stuff that won't die and start rotting. Like I've said in previous chapters, you can't go wrong with Mepps, Rooster Tail or Panther Martin spinners for high lakes. The best colors are yellow, black, silver or gold and spinners with bucktails in a variety of colors. Use small spinners, like something around ⅛ ounces.

For flies, cover yourself by taking floating (dry) and sinking (wet) flies. Nymph and shrimp patterns in black, olive green or gray are sure-fire bets. Any dry flies like an Adams, Mosquito, Renegade, Royal Wulff and Ant will work. These are generalities. Check with local fly shops for what flies are best for high lakes in their regions.

Where To Go

Like I said before, I'm not going to pinpoint lakes with goldens or grayling. There are only so many and sending hordes of anglers to them would put too much pressure on a delicate resource.

If you want to search for these fish, then do your homework and start hiking. You'll find them in certain regions, and I've listed them. Give Fish and Game a call for more details. Have fun looking for them.

Panther Martin Spinner

Rooster Tail

Mepps Aglia®

Ice Fishing

A bobber dances up and down in the hole in the ice. You run up and grab the fishing line, waiting for the right moment to set the hook and pull in a perch, trout or coho. It will be a surprise. But who cares? Whatever will hit your bait, is OK with you. Darn it. Missed the fish.

Then the bobber on a line in another one of your holes in the ice starts bouncing, so you run across the ice to the hole, hoping to set the hook. Running on ice is hard enough. Running when you're all bundled up in winter clothing for ice fishing is crazy. But you waddle across the ice and bend down and grab the other line. Ice fishing can be fun, and when the fish are biting it can be one of the best ways to catch a mess of fish.

There it goes again. The bobber bounces. Bamm! Your reactions are fine-tuned this time and you set the hook. There's something wiggling on the other end. Good, another perch for the skillet.

When it comes to ice fishing, there are two kinds of people. Those who love it and those who think it's the stupidest thing in the world to go out in the middle of the winter and stand on the ice, hoping for a fish to bite. What the critics of ice fishing fail to realize is that after spending an enjoyable day on the ice, absorbing all the winter scenery, you'll be frying up a few fish for dinner. And, that's what counts.

Idaho is blessed with some really good ice fishing waters and when they're frozen over, there's plenty of space for fishing. It seems like there's more elbow room when ice fishing. You're not crowded on the bank.

OK, so you want to get started. You can keep it simple or just go crazy with all kinds of equipment.

What To Use

The basics you'll need for ice fishing are a fishing rod or tip-ups. Tip-ups are hand lines with bells and flags on them especially made for ice fishing. You can also get short fishing rods designed for ice fishing. I really like these because they give you the fight of catching a fish on a fishing rod. Sometimes pulling a fish in with a hand line isn't very sporting. You can make your own tip-ups out of wood, coat hangers, bells or red plastic (for the flag) or buy them in a sporting goods store.

The best thing to do is roam around the lake while you're ice fishing and check out what other anglers are using. Ice fishermen are very innovative when it comes to making their own equipment. Actually, if all you have is a light spinning or bait-casting rod, use it. It will work fine until you figure out what kind of gear you want to get.

One thing you definitely have to have is an ice auger. If anyone tells you that you can chop through the ice with an axe, forget it. A hand auger or a motorized auger makes all the difference in the world, especially when you have to cut several holes in the ice. Some kind of scoop or strainer is needed to scoop the slush out of the ice-fishing hole on cold days. This will keep the hole from freezing over.

Hooks, small sinkers or split shots and bobbers—the stuff you already have in your tackle box—can work in ice fishing. Worms, salmon eggs, corn, cheese, cut-up perch or jigs all catch fish. I like to attach my bait to a small ice-fishing jig or a flutter spoon. The fluttering action of the lure attracts the fish to the bait.

Where To Go

In Idaho, most lakes and reservoirs are open to year-round fishing, so technically, you can go ice fishing in some of the wildest places, if you can get there.

But most sane people stick to the lakes that are fairly accessible by car, snowmobile or on skis. Here are some of my favorite places:

1. Cascade Reservoir: Located 74 miles north of Boise off Highway 55. It has perch, rainbow trout and coho just itching to bite through a hole in the ice. The south end, near the Cascade Golf Course and city park and near Crown Point are all popular places because they are accessible by road in the winter. All you have to do is take the old highway out of Cascade toward the reservoir.

Coho and rainbows can be found close to the surface at the south end. Perch are usually deep, right off the bottom.

Major access points for the north end of the reservoir are gained from turning west off Idaho 55 at Donnelly. The areas include Tamarack Falls at the new fishing bridge, Poison Creek and Medicare Point. It's good to give the north end a try if you're looking for larger rainbows. They tend to run larger up there, some up to 3 pounds. The middle part of the reservoir, especially over the old river channel, can provide a good mix of coho, rainbows and perch fishing.

Access has traditionally been difficult because of the east-west orientation of Sugarloaf Road, which results in rapid snow drifting. The old highway via Day Star Road is plowed and provides more reliable access to the middle part of the reservoir. The road is located off Highway 55, between Cascade and Donnelly. Anglers still have to walk, ski, or snowmobile to their favorite spots, but they will be able to park their vehicles safely. Access to the middle part is also possible along Westside Road, provided drivers use caution and park their vehicles off the roadway where they won't get stuck or block private driveways.

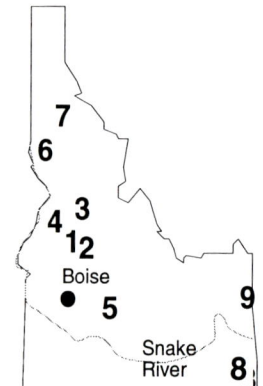

I spent a lot of time talking about Cascade Reservoir because it's one of the best ice-fishing holes around.

2. Horsethief Reservoir: Located about 9 miles east of Cascade off Warm Lake Highway. Drive north out of Cascade on Highway 55 and turn east on the Warm Lake Highway. The cutoff to Horsethief Reservoir is marked. The 3-mile forest road from the highway to the reservoir is usually buried under snow in the winter, which means you've got to ride a snowmobile in. It's a little far for cross-country skiing, especially if you're hauling in a lot of gear.

At Horsethief, you'll catch rainbow trout or splakes (a cross between a female lake trout and a male brook trout). Fish aren't as big as at Cascade Reservoir and range from 8 to 12 inches.

Horsethief is only 275 acres and fishing is only as good as the number of fish that are stocked.

Fishing is usually good when the reservoir first freezes over. As the season progresses it slows down until the ice goes off in spring and the reservoir can be restocked.

3. Little Payette Lake: Located 17 miles north of McCall off the Warren Wagon Road. The road is usually covered with snow and you definitely need a snowmobile to get in. But it's worth it for the rainbow trout and splakes. There are also brook trout that range up to 16 inches in length.

4. Lost Valley Reservoir: Located 16 miles north of Council off U.S. 95. You can take I-84 west of Boise to the Payette exit and travel north through Weiser on U.S. 95 until you get to Council. Keep heading north and turn west at the dirt road at the Pine Ridge Tavern. It's 6 miles to the lake. Sometimes the road to the lake is kept open in winter, sometimes it isn't. When it's snowbound, the best way in is on a snowmobile.

Lost Valley Reservoir has 8 to 20 inch rainbow trout, with most of them averaging 12 to 16 inches. There are some 10 inch splakes roaming around. You'll also catch small perch, but may get lucky and catch a few of the larger fish going 10 to 12 inches. Lost Valley Reservoir is another area where you can get away from the crowds and have a backcountry experience.

5. Magic Reservoir: Located about 20 miles north of Shoshone is another good bet for ice fishing. Take I-84 east out of Boise to the exit at Bliss and take U.S. 26 to Shoshone. From there take Highway 75 north to the reservoir. Look for

signs leading to the reservoir. Magic Reservoir is an excellent fishing spot for rainbow trout and perch. Most of the same fishing methods used at Cascade Reservoir work at Magic.

6. Winchester Lake: Located at Winchester State Park, just off U.S. 95 at Winchester between Grangeville and Lewiston. Winchester Lake is a picturesque spot, especially for ice fishing. The 103-acre lake provides good fishing for stocked rainbow trout.

7. Spring Valley Reservoir: Located about 16 1/2 miles east of Moscow, the 50-acre reservoir offers rainbow trout fishing through the ice. It's a convenient drive from Moscow by taking Highway 8 for 14 miles to Troy and Spring Valley Creek. Then turn north for 2 1/2 miles to the reservoir.

8. Chesterfield Reservoir: The reservoir, located between Pocatello and Soda Springs, is known for its rainbow trout fishing. Located 10 miles north of Bancroft off U.S. Highway 30 on a paved road and then another 4 miles on a dirt road.

9. Palisades Reservoir: This 20-mile reservoir, located on the South Fork of the Snake River on the Idaho-Wyoming border, is known for big fish. They include brown trout, lake trout, kokanee, and cutthroat trout. Scout this reservoir out because it's plenty big. In some spots, it's 185 feet deep.

Reservoir Trout

While deep snow still blankets West Mountain, high above Cascade Reservoir, in March or April the reservoir finally starts to shed its blanket of ice.

First a blue ribbon of water, about 100 feet wide, starts to unravel along the shoreline between the bank and the main chunk of ice in the middle of the reservoir. When this happens, the ice on Cascade Reservoir can be seen disappearing slightly each day. And, then suddenly, if conditions are right, the ice can vanish overnight.

When just a hint of open water begins to sparkle around the lake in spring, shore anglers swarm to the reservoir like ants to bread crumbs. The ritual, which is called ice out, has fishermen lining the reservoir's banks near popular places like the Cascade Golf Course and Sugarloaf Island.

Ice out is a magical time of year when rainbow trout cruise the shoreline of the 30,000-acre reservoir where ice has disappeared. Fish have the urge to spawn and seek the shallow, sandy shorelines. Anglers can have a heyday. Most fishermen sit back in lawn chairs, waiting for a bite. I remember watching one angler who didn't have time to sit, he was having a heyday running to his line and jerking back on the fishing rod. He would immediately reel in a 3-pound, brightly colored rainbow trout. I'll always remember that spring. I just sat there and watched him until finally I had to walk over and ask what the heck he was using for bait. The fisherman simply said, "Steelhead roe."

I'll never forget that day on Cascade Reservoir. While most anglers were using worms and marshmallows, this one guy was catching more fish with a little innovation. He put steelhead roe in a sack made of red thread and secured it to a hook. Then he only threw the line out about 25 feet. He limited out with a bunch of nice rainbows in less than an hour.

Fishing can be fast and furious during ice out, especially if you have the right bait. That doesn't mean that steelhead roe is the only thing to use. I've seen bank anglers nail trout on worms and marshmallows, worms and corn, salmon eggs and even Quaker Puffed Wheat or Quaker Puffed Rice.

What? No, I'm not going loony. One year around ice out at Manns Creek Reservoir I spied an angler using the breakfast cereal that was a favorite of mine when I was a kid. You see, a piece of Puffed Wheat or Puffed Rice looks like a maggot on a hook when floating under water. I hope I don't get sued by the company calling their cereal something akin to a maggot but hey, I gave it a try and it really worked and caught

Worm and marshmallow

a few trout.

Now don't get me wrong. I like Puffed Wheat and Puffed Rice, but so do the trout. You really get some crazy looks when you put a piece on your hook and then put a piece in your mouth. People think you're eating maggots! Well, anyway it tastes good to you and the fish.

What To Use

Worms and marshmallows: This is the bait of choice year-round when fishing a reservoir from the bank. Here's how you make the rig: first cut an 18-inch piece of line off the main line on your fishing rod. Then slip an egg sinker on your main line. To keep the slip sinker from slipping off the line, tie a small barrel swivel on the line by the loop of the swivel. On the other loop of the swivel tie the 18 inches of line. At the end of the 18 inches, tie on a No. 6 hook.

Now take a look at the sinker. It can't go past the swivel, so when you cast it stays 18 inches above the hook. But if you pull on the hook, the line slips through the sinker. You can pull 2 or 3 feet of line through the sinker.

Well, anyway, the point is, a fish can pick up the bait and run with it and won't feel the sinker. But you will know the fish is taking the bait because your line will start running out.

OK, on the hook put a piece of marshmallow first. Then put on a worm. The marshmallow helps keep the worm off the bottom of the reservoir and makes it more attractive to fish. Thus, you've got a marshmallow and worm combination with a slip sinker rig—one of the most common rigs for reservoir fishing in Idaho.

More Combos: You can substitute other baits. Some anglers like salmon eggs and corn, plain single pieces of corn, marshmallows and corn, salmon eggs and corn, or whatever. The secret is the marshmallow because it keeps the rig off the bottom.

Power Bait—Another newcomer on the scene making a hit for reservoir fishing is Berkley's Power Bait. The doughy, cream-like substance can be put on a hook just plain and do the trick. It comes in flavors and it's definitely worth giving a try.

Garlic, etc.: Don't chicken out when it comes to trying other baits. Commercial garlic, cheese baits, anise-flavored cheeses or plain Velveeta Cheese all work as trout bait. The store shelves are stocked with different kinds of baits for reservoir fishing.

Where To Go

1. Cascade Reservoir: This is one of the top reservoirs for bank fishing. It is located 74 miles north of Boise off Highway 55. Give it a try for sure, especially during ice out.

2. Lucky Peak Reservoir: Located about 8 miles east of Boise, Lucky Peak Reservoir is another bank angler's paradise, especially in spring. For some reason fishing gets good around spring break for schools in Boise. Use a marshmallow and worm combo.

3. C.J. Strike Reservoir: Located about 75 miles southeast of Boise, C.J. Strike is well known for bass, perch and crappie fishing. But don't forget this one as a trout fishery. One of the best places to fish from the bank with a marshmallow and worm combo is near the dam. You can reach the reservoir by taking I-84 south of Boise and taking the Simpco Road exit. The back road eventually takes you to the paved highway between Mountain Home and Grand View. Continue to Grand View and to the reservoir.

4. Magic Reservoir: Located about 20 miles north of Shoshone, Magic is well known as a bait-dunker's heaven. Fish around the lower end of the reservoir with a slip-sinker combo and you'll catch fish.

5. Montpelier Reservoir: Located a few miles east of Montpelier on U.S. 89, this reservoir is almost exclusively bank fishing. When this reservoir is stocked, you can try almost anywhere along its banks and catch trout. It's a sure bet and a fun place to fish from spring to fall.

Float Tubes

It must go back to when we were kids. Bobbing in the water in an inner tube is fun and relaxing. Maybe that's why bobbing around in a float tube is such a joy, even if the fish aren't biting.

Float-tube fishing is one of the most relaxing ways to fish. I've never heard of anyone falling asleep in a float tube and being awakened by a trout hitting the line, but it could very easily happen. Just dangling out there in the middle of a lake does wonders for the spirit. It can also do wonders for the creel. Belly boats, fishing donuts, or whatever you want to call them, have revolutionized the sport of fishing. There is no need to drag a boat to your favorite fishing hole and worry about a trailer, fickle lights or long lines at the boat ramp. Just pull your float tube out of the back of the truck or from the car trunk, put on your waders and fins, and launch off the bank.

Float tubes are used for both warm-water species, like bluegill, crappies and bass, or cold-water fishing for trout. You can use them for fly fishing or spin fishing. Belly boats are being redesigned and lightened to the point where you can pack one into a high-mountain lake, blow it up with your mouth, and launch for alpine trout.

Float tubes are also a valuable tool for teaching someone to fly fish. In the middle of a pond, there's practically nothing for a beginner to get snagged on while casting. The novice fly angler doesn't have to worry about what is in back of him or her. And, what beats all is that trout practically hook themselves as the beginner fly angler drags a nymph behind the tube. It's just like trolling lures from a boat, although purist fly anglers don't want to admit it. Anyway, fishing from a float tube gives the novice a lot of confidence and helps them advance in the sport.

While float tubes are relaxing, they also offer a very good low-impact way of exercising. I'm not kidding. Float-tube anglers are constantly wiggling their legs to get around a pond or lake, troll a reservoir or maneuver into position for a good cast. After a few hours of float tubing, you'll feel it in your legs. It's great that such a fun activity as fishing could do so much in promoting exercise and health.

And you can float tube practically year-round in Idaho, depending on the weather. With the advent of light, warm synthetic clothing, it is possible now to use a float tube in the winter. Just put on a pair of polypro longjohns and a pair of polar-type fleece pants under a pair of neoprene waders and you're all set. Cover your upper body with polypro longjohns, a fleece pullover and a wind jacket. You'll find float-tube fishermen on waters in some of the milder spots in Idaho throughout the winter.

Now that I've sold you on float-tube fishing let's talk about some of the best places to go and a few of the best flies and lures.

What To Use

Flies: OK, the easiest way to catch a trout out of a float tube is to tie on a Stayner Ducktail, Canadian Brown Leech, Sheep Creek Special, Woolly Bugger, or plain old Woolly Worm.

Line: You'll have to experiment on depth until you find where the fish are, but in most cases a sinking fly line is best. If it's early in the spring, or if the trout have just been stocked in

the pond, most likely you'll find trout feeding near the surface. I use a floating line in this situation and drag it about 25 to 30 yards behind the tube.

If it's mid-summer and the water's warmer, you might have to go deeper and that will take sinking fly line. It also depends on the lake or reservoir itself. Ask local anglers for tips on the types of fly lines they use.

Lures: Spin fishermen also use float tubes. You can fish spinners, spoons or jigs from a float tube. In fact, any lures you use from a boat will work in a float tube.

Where To Go

Float tubers in Idaho are lucky. There are plenty of places to try, and you'll find a variety of fish. Here are a few favorites:

1. Horsethief Reservoir: Located about 8 miles east of Cascade, this reservoir is float-tubing heaven. The reservoir is stocked with trout and offers some of the best fly fishing around. To get there drive 74 miles north of Boise on Highway 55 and turn east on the Warm Lake Highway, just past Cascade. Drive 6 miles to Horsethief Reservoir Road on the south and travel about 3 miles to the reservoir.

2. Brownlee Reservoir : Located just north of Weiser on the Snake River, this reservoir is one of the best places to catch crappie and bass from a float tube. The coves of the reservoir are hideaways for good fishing. Get a few Stayner Ducktails, Woolly Buggers or Jigs and you're on your way to hooking some fish. One thing though, Brownlee is a big reservoir and the winds can stir up ocean-like waves. Float tubers should stay in the small coves and never venture out in open water. To get to Brownlee Reservoir, take I-84 from Boise to the Payette exit and continue north on U.S. 95 to Weiser. At Weiser, you can take the Old Ferry Road to Brownlee Reservoir. Drive along the old road until you find a place to fish. Or, you can continue on U.S. 95 to Cambridge and then take Highway 71 west to the lower end of Brownlee Reservoir.

3. Paddock Reservoir: Located about 70 miles north of Boise, Paddock has long been crappie heaven for float tubers. The reservoir has had major setbacks in crappie fishing because of the drought of the late '80s and early '90s, but it should, hopefully, make a major comeback in the '90s. Let's hope so. Fish with Woolly Buggers, Woolly Worms or jigs and you'll get lucky with the crappie. To get there, take Highway 52 from Emmett to Payette. Just 6 miles before you hit Payette, take a north turn on the Little Willow Road. Drive about 20 miles to the end of the road and there's Paddock Reservoir. It's a rough drive but worth it.

4. Sagehen Reservoir: This a float-tuber's paradise, as far as scenery is concerned. The reservoir is stocked with trout and one of southwest Idaho's most popular fishing and camping spots. It has full-service Forest Service campgrounds and a boat ramp. Oh, who needs a boat ramp with a float tube, right? To get to Sagehen, travel on Highway 53 between Horseshoe Bend and Emmett. At Ola, take a turn to the north and go 18 miles to the reservoir.

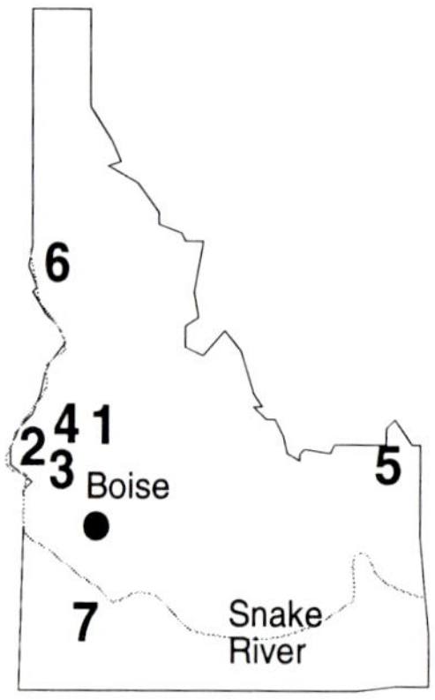

5. Henry's Lake: Idaho's float-tube navy converges on Henry's Lake in eastern Idaho every summer. Henry's Lake is known for its trophy cutthroat, hybrid and brook trout. It is reached by driving north out of Idaho Falls on U.S. 20. It is a popular lake, too, because of its proximity to the Yellowstone area.

6. Winchester Lake: Located at Winchester State Park, just off U.S. Highway 95 at the town of Winchester, south of Lewiston. The lake is picturesque and ideal for float tubing. It's also stocked with trout which makes it a likely spot for beginners. It is reached by driving U.S. 95 and turning west to Winchester, between Grangeville and Lewiston.

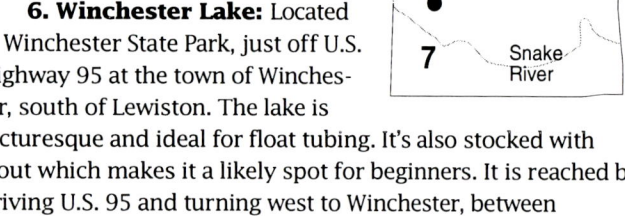

7. Crane Falls Reservoir: If there was ever a spot to start off beginners in float-tube fishing, it's Crane Falls Reservoir, located south of Mountain Home. The small lake mainly has bluegills, trout and bass. The lake is stocked with trout and is one of the earliest places for fishing in the spring. When the bluegills are on their spawning beds, it's one of the most fun places to fish from a float tube. The reservoir is reached by driving 17 miles south of Mountain Home on Highway 51 and turning west on a gravel road for 8 miles.

Stream Fishing For Trout

In all my days of fishing, I'd never come up on a fish truck dumping a load of trout in a stream and been able to cast a line. So I never had the opportunity to answer the age-old question: How long does it take for a trout to bite after it is stocked? Well, one summer it finally happened. I was driving down Trail Creek Road near Ketchum, Idaho, and there it was plain as day.

An Idaho Department of Fish and Game tanker had just dumped a whole bunch of wiggling rainbows in Trail Creek. I tried to act cool and calm as I screeched on the brakes and sent up a cloud of dust as my four-wheel-drive rig, Old Red, ripped up the highway shoulder. After fish-tailing my rig in the parking area, I tried to look as ho-hum as possible waiting for the tanker to leave.

Actually, I was ready to grab my fishing rod faster than Wyatt Earp could draw his six-shooter at the OK Corral. The fish truckers were probably laughing their heads off at the flatlander with Ada County license plates who was just itching to get to those rainbows. The puddles from the fish truck were still fresh on the pavement as I grabbed my fly rod and tied a brown Renegade to my line. A Renegade usually comes with white hackle on one end of the peacock body and brown on the other end. I like brown on both sides.

I casually strolled toward the creek as if I didn't know anything about the fish truck. But in all seriousness, I was conducting a very scientific experiment.

An important question had to be answered and somebody had to do it. Ha!, you say, old Zimowsky was probably drooling like an Alaskan brown bear about to wade into a stream full of bright-red salmon. No way. I was acting very professional about it. I only tripped over my feet twice.

Sneaking up to the stream bank, I caught an amazing sight. The hatchery trout were already coming to the surface looking for dinner. They were breaking water like sharks in a feeding frenzy. Don't they feed these critters at the hatchery? What a great idea. Starve them a few days before they're released and they'll hit anything. That way fishing will be fantastic and nobody will complain to the Fish and Game.

Boy oh boy, I couldn't wait any longer. Being so nervous with the important study I was about to conduct, my first cast hooked a tree limb. Get that darn thing untangled. Here it is, the moment of truth. I flipped out the Renegade and as soon as it hit the water, a trout nailed it. Three minutes from the truck to my line. In about 10 minutes, I must have caught-and-released more than a dozen rainbows. I had to finally give up because the fly came unraveled.

I didn't even have a cooler in the car to take home a few for dinner. The one time I get a break and it doesn't do any good. But what's more important, the question of how long

does it take for a trout to hit after it's been stocked has been answered—No time at all.

What To Use

OK, what do you use for stream fishing, especially one with stocked rainbow trout? You've got a lot of options:

• Small spinners, such as yellow Rooster Tails, Mepps Black Fury or yellow Panther Martins are the ticket. Small-stream trout love them. Be careful fishing spinners in small streams or you'll spook the fish. Sneak around tree limbs and boulders, gently casting the spinner across the stream, reeling slowly and letting it drift downstream as you retrieve it.

• Another rig that used to be popular when I was younger, but I don't hear too much about now, is the Colorado spinner and a worm. It can be fished by allowing it to drift downstream and retrieving it slowly. This works especially well in small streams lined with brushy banks where casting is difficult. It's dynamite in streams with deep holes, too. Sneak up to a deep hole and gently cast the spinner and worm

over it toward the back end of the pool. Let it settle toward the bottom and slowly reel in. Be ready for the strike, especially from the big ones hiding under the cut banks covered with heavy brush. Oh, by the way, the Colorado spinner can also be fished with a salmon egg as bait.

• Flies are usually fool-proof on small streams. Some basic patterns to use are the regular Renegade with brown and white hackle, the brown Renegade with all brown hackle, Royal Wulff, Gray Hackle Peacock, Joe's Hopper (or other type of hopper fly), any small caddis pattern, or the Stayner Ducktail. Believe it or not, once while fishing on the Middle Fork of the Boise River, about 6 miles above Arrowrock Reservoir, the only fly that would work was a Stayner Ducktail. It must have represented a stonefly nymph. It took several whitefish and nice-sized trout.

Where To Go

Idaho has miles and miles of small streams that are often ignored by anglers. Check regulations on certain sections of streams to make sure you can use bait. Some rivers may only allow artificial lures and flies only, with a single barbless hook.

Here are some of my favorite small streams:

1. The Middle Fork of the Payette River, north of Crouch. You get to it by driving north of Boise on Highway 55 to Banks and turning east on the Banks to Lowman Highway until you get to the turnoff to Crouch. Head north and follow the river until you see a few holes you want to fish. I've done really well with both spinners and flies on this stream.

2. South Fork of the Boise River (above Anderson Ranch Reservoir). This is one of my favorite small streams for fly fishing. Drive north out of Mountain Home on Highway 20 to the cutoff for Pine and Featherville. Fish the South Fork in this area.

3. The Boise River Let's not forget the river right in downtown Boise. It's easily reached along the Boise Greenbelt and at places like Broadway, Americana and Glenwood bridges and at Barber Park. Spinners, flies and bait work well in this stream. Don't forget to try salmon eggs along this stretch, sometimes they are the only thing that works.

4. Trail Creek, located right out of Ketchum on Trail Creek Road, is a good stream that's well stocked with trout. It's great for fly fishing. It is easily reached northeast of Ketchum.

5. The Upper Salmon River near Stanley is a choice stream for trout fishing, when the river is stocked with rainbows. Spinners are the best method of fishing these waters. Flies are another good choice. Fishing with lures and flies is so much fun in this stretch of river, I've never had to resort to bait. The river is easily reached by driving about 125 miles northeast of Boise on Highway 21 to Stanley. From there, turn either northeast or south on Highway 75 and pick out a spot that looks good to you.

Trolling for Trout, Coho and Kokanee

Trolling has to be one of the most relaxing ways to fish. And, most of the time, the fish hooks itself. You can just sit back in the boat, listen to the hum of the engine, and enjoy the scenery. When your rod tip suddenly bends toward the water, you can set the hook, and reel in the fish.

You don't have to have a big fancy motorboat for trolling. But it helps, especially on big reservoirs. On smaller lakes, you can get by with a rowboat, canoe or float tube. My kids learned how to troll in our canoe. I'd just put a Mepps or Rooster Tail on their lines, sit them in the canoe, and paddle around a small lake, like Horsethief Reservoir, Warm Lake or Sagehen Reservoir. It's great for youngsters. All they have to do is sit there and wait for the trout to hook on their line. We spent a lot of fun days paddling around lakes hooking into small rainbows.

Spring or early summer is an ideal time for trolling because the water is cool on the surface and you don't have to go deep to get to the fish. This means you can just put a spinner or lure on the end of your line and drag it from behind the boat. In late summer, when reservoir or lake waters are warm on top, you have to go down deep for trout, coho or kokanee. That means using leaded line and pop gear. Pop gear is a series of flashers that attract fish.

What To Use

Spinners: By far, Mepps, Rooster Tail, Blue Fox, Vibrax or Panther Martin spinners are ideal for trolling.

Plugs: Small Flatfish and Rapalas are good bets. I like the yellow Flatfish with red and black spots and the silver blue Rapala, which looks like a small bait fish.

Spoons: Little Cleos, Dardevle, Kastmasters,

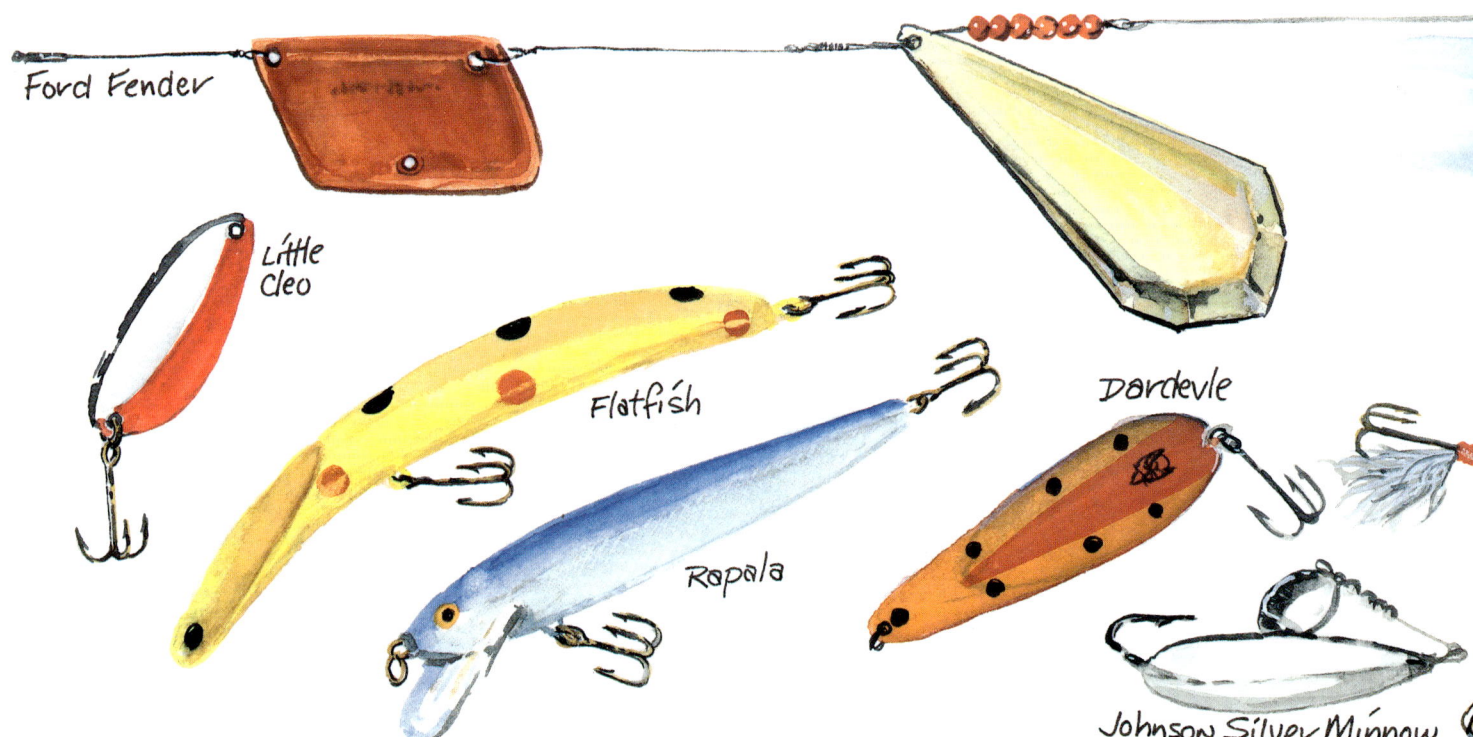

Krocodile and Johnson Silver Minnows are all good choices.
Flies—Stayner Ducktails, Canadian Brown Leeches, Woolly Buggers and Woolly Worms can work just as well as lures.

Bait: Dead minnows, worms, and salmon eggs can be put on the end of a Wedding Ring spinner with pop gear and can be deadly when trolling deep in summer for coho or kokanee.

Pop Gear: Trolling gear, like flashers, is used to get down deep for trout and kokanee. Ford Fenders and Beer Cans are only a few of the brands of flashers for trolling. A popular trolling rig is a Ford Fender with a Wedding Ring spinner with a worm on it. Some anglers substitute a Woolly Worm or other leech-type fly, a salmon egg or piece of corn for the worm.

Where To Go

1. Lucky Peak Reservoir: This reservoir is best in spring and fall. In fact, fall fishing can be incredible all the way into November. Summer is best left to the waterskiers and speedboaters. The reservoir is reached by taking Highway 21, 8 miles east of Boise. Although I've used the canoe in Lucky Peak up in the narrows near Macks Creek, a motorboat is recommended. It's too big a reservoir for a canoe.

2. Arrowrock Reservoir: This is another good spring water for trolling. By mid-summer, it starts to get pretty low for trolling. The reservoir is located upstream from Lucky Peak Reservoir and is often ignored by Boise fishermen.

3. Cascade Reservoir: Known for its coho salmon and rainbow trout fishing, this reservoir is a sure bet for trollers. Early spring right after ice out can be excellent. Basically, it's good all season long until it freezes up in December.

This is another large reservoir that should be fished with a motorboat. The winds can kick up pretty bad and send swells across the reservoir. Cascade Reservoir is located 74 miles north of Boise on Highway 55 at the town of Cascade.

4. Sagehen Reservoir: This is a favorite of mine. It can be fished from a canoe or float tube. It is stocked all summer long and usually is a good bet, especially for kids. The reservoir is reached by driving 18 miles north of Triangle off Highway 52 between Horseshoe Bend and Emmett.

5. Warm Lake: This is another good bet for trolling in a canoe or row boat. It has rainbow trout and kokanee. The lake is located about 25 miles east of Cascade on Warm Lake Highway.

6. Anderson Ranch Reservoir: A favorite among trollers at Anderson Ranch Reservoir are the kokanee. Fishermen go after kokanee all summer long, but there's a point in the summer when the fish start circling the reservoir just before they go up the tributaries to spawn that fishing can be excellent.

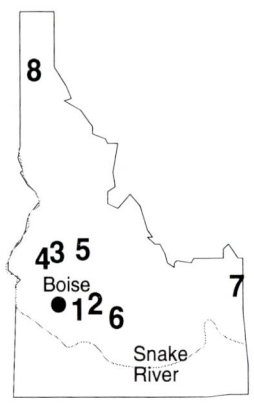

Anderson Ranch Reservoir is located about 70 miles east of Boise. Take the freeway to Mountain Home and then Highway 20 to the Anderson Ranch Dam cutoff.

7. Island Park Reservoir: If you're taking a vacation to Yellowstone, a stop-off at this reservoir is a must. It can provide excellent fishing for a variety of trout and also kokanee salmon. The reservoir is located 25 miles north of Ashton on Highway 20.

8. Pend Oreille Lake: Nothing even comes close to hooking on to one of Idaho's famous Kamloops trout. The prized fish lure anglers from all over the state. The largest lake in Idaho is located near the town of Sandpoint. The lake also has kokanee, rainbow trout and a variety of other fish.

Wild About Whitefish

I'm wild about whitefish. OK, that sounds dumb. The lowly mountain whitefish doesn't have a chance in purist rainbow-trout country. It's got a mouth like a sucker and a body like a cigar, so anglers think it's a trash fish.

About 84 percent of the people who buy fishing licenses in Idaho fish for trout. Only 10 percent cast a line for whitefish. What's worse is, whitefish are blamed for taking over living space inhabited by trout and even for taking food right out of their mouths. That's too bad. Whitefish are a game fish. There are plenty of fishermen who consider whitefish a treasure for winter fishing and a delicacy fresh out of the smoker.

Frankly, in the winter, if a trout gets on my line, it's an inconvenience. It's fun to fish for whitefish because there's a liberal limit and you can fill the freezer. A good-size whitefish will also put up a good fight, especially on a fly rod. Another thing, even though some streams are closed to trout fishing during winter, they're still open for whitefishing.

The taste of smoked whitefish and the sport of catching dozens each trip has lured me to places like the South Fork of the Boise River, the Middle Fork of the Boise River and the South Fork of the Payette River for years. I'll go to any length to catch a bucket of whitefish, even driving 25 miles up the cliff-hanger, muddy, rock-strewn road that follows along the Middle Fork of the Boise River.

On a warm February day, places like the South Fork of the Payette River can be beautiful. The river is usually low and clear and you can see the bottom, which resembles a cobblestone street. If you look close enough, you can see the flash of a whitefish feeding just off the bottom.

The hardest part about whitefishing is learning how to keep your rig on the bottom of the stream, whether you're using bait or flies. Once you learn how to do that, and learn how to feel the light bite of a whitefish, you've got it made. You'll never again have to put your fishing rod away, just because it's winter.

What To Use

Max Berry's Whitefish Rig—Invented by Boisean, Max Berry, this fool-proof rig makes it easy to fish for whitefish.

It's a little complicated so let's take it slow. First, get 18 inches of monofilament line. At one end tie a pencil sinker with rubber tubing between it and the line. In the top end of the rubber tubing, insert a barrel swivel and wrap line around it to hold it inside the tubing. Attach your line to the loop of the swivel, which is outside the tubing. On the other end of the tubing, insert a pencil sinker. You can get them where steelhead fishing gear is sold.

Next attach another piece of monofilament about 9 inches up the line. To the end of this piece of line, tie a small fly, like the Tanned Deer Skin fly. At the end of the 18 inches of monofilament, tie on a rubber band. Yup, a rubber band. Attach the end of the rubber band to the swivel on your main fishing line leading to your rod. The rubber band keeps constant pressure on the line when you're fighting a whitefish, especially when a barbless hook is involved. Cast it upstream and let it drift to a hole.

Fly fishing for whitefish can be very rewarding. In the Boise River, whitefish prefer small flies. An excellent choice is the No. 14 Green Caddis Larvae. For larger rivers that have stoneflies, try the George's Brown Stonefly Nymph in sizes No. 8 through 14. This is a good one for the South Fork of the Boise River or the South Fork of the Payette River. A Bead-Head Hare's Ear Nymph is also a good choice for all three rivers. Use a small one for the Boise River.

In the Boise River, the best areas are right below the riffles, especially in low water. Look for the nice runs, about 3 to 5 feet deep, in other rivers.

Another whitefish rig, which is effective when fishing off a bridge or out of a boat, is a simple sinker tied to the end of the line with two hooks. Place the hooks at points about 10 inches and 20 inches up the line.

Another simple whitefish rig is to tie a hook on the end of the line and put a couple of small split shots about 12 to 18 inches up the line. On all bait rigs, use small grubs or maggots. You can also turn over rocks in the river and use natural baits like stonefly nymphs

Whitefish Rig

Where To Go

1. South Fork of the Boise River: Located about 70 miles southeast of Boise, the South Fork has consistently been one of the best areas for whitefish. It is reached from Boise in about 1 1/2 hours by taking I-84 east from Boise to the Fairfield exit at Mountain Home. Continue north on U.S. 20 to the turn off to Anderson Ranch Dam. Fish the river below. It is a special regulation trout water so check Idaho's fishing rules for details.

2. Middle Fork of the Boise River: The stretch of river upstream from Arrowrock Reservoir is a very good whitefishing river. It's uncrowded during winter because access is difficult. Basically, you've got 25 miles of bad road to get to the river and that discourages fishermen, especially in winter. To get there, take Idaho 21 northeast out of Boise to the Mores Creek Bridge and turn east on the Middle Fork of the Boise River.

3. Boise River: You can catch plenty of whitefish in the Boise River right through town. Some of the best places are near Barber Park and Municipal Park.

4. South Fork of the Payette River: This section of river is closed to trout fishing in winter, but has great fishing for whitefish. Some of the best places are in Garden Valley and around Lowman. Take Highway 55 north from Boise to Banks and turn east toward Garden Valley.

Bass

When a bass slams your line and blasts out of the water like a missile fired from a submarine, look out. You know you're in for a fight.

Maybe that's why smallmouth and largemouth bass are some of America's favorite fish. They are favorites among Idahoans, too.

Bass are powerful fish and will take a graphite rod and bend it like a piece of spaghetti.Bass like warm water. They grow faster in warm lakes, reservoirs and rivers. In a reservoir like C.J. Strike in southern Idaho, where the weather is warmer than northern Idaho, it takes less than three years for a bass to reach 12 inches. But up north in a place like Hauser Lake, it takes seven years for a bass to reach that size.

It's important to fish warmer waters so you'll catch large bass. Warm waters are those at low and mid elevations around farmlands and desert canyons. You won't find bass in a cold, clear rushing high mountain stream. That's why bass fall into the category called warm-water fish.

There are two kinds of bass in Idaho, smallmouth and largemouth.Largemouth are dark green on the back and sides and have white bellies. They like still-water, such as farm ponds, lakes and

skinhead™

PLASTIC WORMS

sloughs. You'll even find largemouth bass in ponds in the middle of Boise. Largemouths like to hide under lily pads, in weeds and under overhanging branches.

Their cousins, smallmouth bass, have a dark olive-brown back, bronze sides and reddish eyes. They also have white bellies, Smallmouths like moving water. You'll find them in low-elevation rivers, such as the Snake, Payette and Boise rivers hanging around the points of islands and rocky cliffs. In reservoirs you'll find them along rocky shorelines and coves.

What To Use

Talk to local fishing shops to find out what they're hitting. Here are some popular lures for Idaho waters:

The Gitzit is a good all-around lure that should be fished on a lead-head jig. Used for fishing deep-water breaks or on the bottom and good in spring or fall when fish are sluggish. Cast it out, let it free-fall or reel in slowly so it crawls along the bottom.

The Plastic Ringworm is a jigging or floating-type lure used just off the bottom in a jerking action. The Plastic Worm is a popular lure that is also used for jigging.

Crankbaits are plugs, which look like minnows or crayfish, they are designed to go to certain depths. Cast them out and reel them in,

the wiggling action attracts fish. They are effectively used by bumping them against the bottom, disturbing the mud like crayfish, and getting fish to bite. Spinnerbaits are another top-water lure, used to fish tight spots. Cast it out and let it fall to the bottom, as it falls it produces a helicopter motion. A plastic worm or pork rind can be added as an attractor.

The Buzzbait is used for top-water fishing and is good early in the morning when bass are feeding. It has a crazy-looking blade that spins as the lure is reeled in. The blade makes a splash in the water, sort of like one of the beaters on an electric cake mixer. The noise also attracts fish.

Lead-Head Jigs are rigged with plastic worms and tube lures. The heavier the jig, the deeper it will take the lure down. Embedding the jig hook in the plastic worm will keep the lure from getting snagged in the weeds.

Where To Go

Bass really start biting in April and southwestern Idaho has plenty of places to cast a line for them. Here are some best bets:

1. Anderson Ranch Reservoir: A 5,000-acre reservoir on the South Fork of the Boise River. Good in late spring, summer and fall. Fishing is good in the coves, especially where streams flow into the reservoir. Accessible north from Mountain Home on Highway 20. About 2 1/2 hours from Boise.

2. Brownlee Reservoir: A 15,000-acre reservoir located on the Snake River near Weiser. Good from March to October with a lull during late July and August. Best fishing is near rocky structures along the shoreline and in the coves. Accessible off I-84 near Huntington, Oregon, Old Ferry Road north of Weiser, or on Highway 71, west of Cambridge. About 1 1/2 to 2 1/2 hours from Boise.

3. Oxbow Reservoir: A 1,500-acre reservoir located just downstream from Brownlee Reservoir. Good during the same season as Brownlee. Accessible by taking the same road from Cambridge. About 3 hours from Boise.

4. Hells Canyon Reservoir: A 2,500-acre reservoir located downstream from Oxbow Reservoir. Good during the same season as Brownlee and Oxbow. Take the same route as Oxbow. About 3 1/2 hours from Boise.

5. C.J. Strike Reservoir: A 7,500-acre reservoir, accessible between Grand View and Bruneau on Highway 78. Good in May, the best fishing is during April, May and June. Fall fishing can be good in September and October. About 1 1/2 hours from Boise.

6. Snake River: The river from Hagerman to Brownlee Reservoir and through Hells Canyon to Lewiston. The smallmouth bass fishing in Hells Canyon is some of the best in Idaho.

7. Lake Lowell: A 10,000-acre lake, located just south of Nampa. Best in the summer months. Take Lake Lowell Avenue west from Nampa to the upper dam boat ramp. About 35 to 40 minutes from Boise.

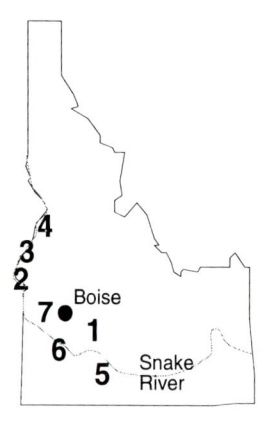

Bluegills

I was skeptical. A bait dealer had just sold me a dozen crickets and guaranteed they'd catch a whole mess of bluegills. For the same price, I could have gotten a couple of candy bars and dug up some worms in my backyard. Well, what the heck, I thought I'd give the crickets a try.

The closest place to test my new box of chirpers was Duff Lane Pond, a small pond along the Boise River between Star and Middleton. The pond was packed with bluegills and a sure-fire test for the crickets. If only the darn things would quit chirping. The things chirp so loud, they have been known to set off alarm systems in bait stores.

I put the cricket on a small No. 12 hook rigged with a bobber. A small split shot between the hook and the bobber added a little weight. The bobber wasn't in the water 10 seconds before it started bouncing up and down. Soon it disappeared under water and a bluegill was darting back and forth trying to bust loose.

I'll never forget Duff Lane and the crickets. It made me realize how easy it is to catch bluegills. And, how much fun. Bluegills are scrappy, they're abundant, and good to eat. What more can you ask for. Big things come in small packages, so to speak.

The neatest thing about bluegills is that you can catch them on a kid's Zebco Snoopy bait-casting outfit, with a bobber and a worm (or a cricket), or a high-priced fly rod. Bluegills give both youngsters and adults a lot of excitement. If you want to take kids out on their first fishing trip, and make it meaningful, just find a bluegill pond. They're great sport and many ponds throughout Idaho have them. You can go after them from the bank, in a boat, or in a float tube.

The best time to fish for bluegills is late May and early June when they're spawning. If the water is clear and you can see down to the bottom, the nests look like craters on the moon. Females deposit their eggs in the nests and the males guard them. That's when the males will strike at almost anything and fishing can be fantastic.

The good thing about bluegills is that there are no bag limits on most waters. Bluegills are so prolific, they usually overpopulate a pond or

lake. When that happens, bluegills get stunted and they all end up tiny. When you catch a lot of them and reduce their numbers, there is more food for other fish. The remaining fish will grow larger

What To Use

Bobber and Worm: Put a small, round bobber on the end of your line. About 18 inches below the bobber, tie on a No. 12 or 14 hook. The bobber can be moved up and down, depending on how deep the bluegills are.

Add a small garden worm to the hook, not a big piece of nightcrawler but a small red worm found in your garden. You can also use crickets or grubs on the hook.

Flies: The best flies for bluegills are small nymphs. Bluegills aren't fussy about fly patterns. Small Woolly Worms or Woolly Buggers work great. Dark colors, such as brown, black, green, gray or olive are preferred. A floating spider fly can be a killer when bluegills are coming to the surface.

Where To Go

If you want to try bluegill fishing, here are a few good spots in southwest Idaho:

1. Crane Falls Reservoir: Bluegill fishing can be dynamite when the fish are spawning in the shallow, weedy areas around the lake. Fishing is usually good in June. The reservoir is reached by driving 17 miles south of Mountain Home on Idaho 51. Continue past the bridge over the Snake River. Up the hill and on the right will be a sign pointing to Crane Falls Reservoir. It's about 8 miles off the highway on the edge of the Snake River.

2. Boise River Ponds: Many of the ponds along the Boise River have bluegills. Park Center Pond, Veterans Pond, and ponds near Glenwood Bridge in the Boise area are good bets.

3. Duff Lane Pond: This pond near Star is another good choice. My kids learned about bluegill fishing here. Duff Lane is reached 1 mile southeast of Middleton off Idaho 44.

4. Caldwell Ponds: These two ponds in Canyon County are great spots for float-tubing for bluegills. Take the Parma exit on I-84 just west of Caldwell. One mile past the junction is a Sportsman's Access sign to the left. Turn off the road and you'll find the ponds.

5. Bruneau Sand Dunes Lakes: The lakes at Bruneau Dunes State Park, are known for bluegill fishing. It's a good spot for a float-tube or canoe. In summer you'll find bluegills up against the shore in the weeds. If you're a wading fisherman, you can walk out into the shallow waters and cast back toward the bank and catch bluegills. Kids can catch them from the bank with a bobber and worm.

The good thing about the Sand Dunes Lakes is that if fishing is slow, the kids will keep occupied climbing the dunes. You get to the state park by driving to Mountain Home on I-84 and then driving about 16 miles south on Idaho 51. Turn east on Idaho 78, just across the Snake River and go about two miles to the park's entrance.

Floating Spider Fly

Bobber and Worm

Woolly Bugger

Catfish

Catfish fillets simmered in a Dutch oven, bubbling in Cajun sauce. A gang of hungry river runners circled the oven like a bunch of sharks. The hot coals in the fire pan in our camp along the Snake River in Hells Canyon were the perfect temperature to keep the fillets sizzling and popping in the sauce. The spicy Cajun seasoning sent an aroma flowing through the camp just below Wild Sheep Rapids.

By now the sun was falling below the rim of the deepest canyon in North America. After a day of chukar hunting and fishing in famed Hells Canyon, who could blame the rafters for being hungry. It was your typical cast-and-blast trip.

Next to the Dutch oven were rainbow trout browning on the grill. They looked pretty scrumptious, too. The canyon was providing a banquet of chukars, trout and catfish. When the time came for the taste test, the catfish disappeared faster than you could swamp a raft in the canyon's giant rapids, Granite Falls. The trout were good eating, but the catfish, wow! Especially Cajun blackened catfish. It was out of this world.

It's kind of funny that you could be floating one of the world's most beautiful canyons, shooting at cagey chukars, fishing for brawny rainbow trout and taking in all the wild scenery, and the thing that sticks most in your mind is the taste of catfish. But hey, catfish are good eating. Idaho is known for trout fishing, but few ever associate the "cutthroat trout state" with catfish.

In the travel brochures you see fly fishermen standing waist deep in a mountain trout stream casting for rainbows, not an angler standing in mud along the Snake River putting garlic cheese on a hook. We were so interested in catching bass and trout in Hells Canyon that we didn't even give catfish a thought. Too bad, we almost missed a super dinner.

When we beached the boats that evening and set up camp, we only had chukars and trout. That was fine, except for a Midwesterner in the group. He thought we should have catfish. The next thing we knew he was casting a line in a back eddy on the river, trying for whiskered fish. All he did was put a glob of worms on a hook, weigh it down with a good sinker and let the rig bounce along the bottom of the hole. In no time he hauled in three nice channel catfish. Boy, he converted a lot of trout fishermen that day. OK, now that I've whet your appetite for catfish, let's talk about how to get them.

The Snake River in southwest Idaho and in Hells Canyon is the state's catfishing paradise. From February to November you'll find someone out there bouncing bait on the bottom to nail a catfish.

Channel catfish are the primary catfish most anglers are after. But Idaho also has bullhead, flathead and blue catfish. Most channel cats are taken on bait but they have also been taken on spinners and flies.

What To Use

Make it simple—hook, line, sinker and bait.

Worms are a good choice, especially large nightcrawlers. The best bait is a dead minnow. I say dead minnow because it is illegal to fish in Idaho with live minnows. There are fears that live minnows will escape and grow up to be trash fish in Idaho's waters and take over the food and living space of game fish.

You can catch catfish on a variety of stink baits — concoctions that you make up yourself, such as rotting chicken livers, etc. A variety of cheese baits and other types of soft baits are available commercially. One example is Berkley's Power Bait for catfish. Rad is a secret bait that is available in southwest Idaho at grocery stores, bait shops and convenience stores. It is the spinal cord of a cow. Sounds yucky, but catfish love it. Another good bait in late summer are grasshoppers. Put several on one hook.

Here's another good bait, if you can afford it—raw shrimp from the deli at your favorite grocery store. Catfish love them, that's if you can get them to the fishing hole before someone boils them up for dinner.

No matter what kind of bait you use, one of the simplest rigs is just a hook, sinker and bait. Slip a one-half to one-ounce (slip) egg sinker on your line. The sinker has a hole in it and will travel up and down your line. Next, tie on a barrel swivel 18 inches up the line next to the egg sinker. The swivel will keep your sinker from traveling all the way down the line to the hook. Next comes the hook. Make it a No. 2 hook, one big enough for the big mouths of catfish.

OK, let's see how this crazy-looking rig works. When you cast it out, the swivel prevents the sinker from coming all the way down the line to your hook. When the line is on the bottom, the sinker remains 18 inches away from the bait. The sinker will bounce or stay put on the bottom while the bait drifts naturally off the bottom. When a fish takes the bait, the line flows through the sinker and the fish doesn't get wise because there isn't any drag from the sinker.

Where To Go

1. Snake River: C.J. Strike Dam downstream to the back waters of Brownlee Reservoir includes some of the best catfishing in the river. This is moving water with pools, rapids and eddies. Lots of times you'll find catfish on the bottom in the runs right below the rapids. Eddies are a good part of the river, too. They form part of the river that forms a pool at the bottom of a set of rapids. The water in the eddy is going in the opposite direction as the water in the main body of the river. Usually if you let your bait drift on the bottom upstream in the eddy, you'll find catfish.

2. Brownlee Reservoir: The Snake River flows into Brownlee Reservoir just downstream from Weiser. The southern part or upstream end of the reservoir is known for good catfishing.

You'll see lots of boats anchored where the river starts pooling up in the reservoir, just upstream from Farewell Bend State Park on the Oregon side of the river. You'll also find good catfishing in the area of Steck Park, north of Weiser on the Old Ferry Road.

Bank fishermen usually do well in the Steck Park area. To get to the Oregon side of the reservoir, drive I-84 from Idaho into Oregon. Continue out of Ontario to the Farewell Bend State Park exit. You can also go to Huntington, Oregon, and get to the west side of Brownlee from there.

3. Oxbow Reservoir: This is another reservoir, just downstream from Brownlee Dam, that also has a lot of catfish. If you're an Idaho angler, you'll need a boat. Most of the access is on the Oregon side of the river where the highway runs. But you can camp at McCormick Park on the Idaho side just below Brownlee and fish there. You can also take a boat and fish anywhere on the reservoir.

4. Hells Canyon: Rafters and jet-boaters can find some really good catfishing in the canyon below Hells Canyon Dam all the way to Pittsburgh Landing. The remote canyon offers lots of hideaways for catfish.

Just remember, don't get so involved with catching bass and trout that you forget about Old Mister Whiskers.

Crappie

Catch one and you'll catch more. Ask any old crappie fisherman for sage advice and that's what you'll get. Crappie travel in schools, and that makes for a certain kind of excitement searching for them. There can be a bunch right along the pilings of a dock, or near the rubble of a rocky shoreline, or down below a lone bush out in the middle of the lake. And, when the fishing's good, you can catch hundreds of them, maybe one every few minutes.

Besides hot-and-heavy action, you'll get enough to pack away a lot of fillets in the freezer so you can enjoy fish fries throughout the winter.

Crappies are fun, too, because they have a certain feel. You could be fishing in a lake or reservoir with bass, trout and crappies swimming around, but you automatically know when a crappie hits. It's like a lightning bolt, vibrating like shock waves at the end of the line. It'll dive deep and zig zag all over the place. That's why crappies can be super fun on light spinning gear, a fly rod or even a simple cane pole. It's no wonder that anglers travel hundreds of miles to places like Brownlee Reservoir to catch buckets and buckets of them. This precious little fish attracts hard-core anglers in bass boats and float tubes, packing hundreds of dollars worth of gear or young Huck Finns with Zebco fishing sets dangling a worm and bobber off a dock.

Crappies are a good fish to get someone started in the sport of fishing. If the action is good, you'll hook an angler for life, especially a youngster. Crappies in Idaho start to become active in late April. The month of May seems to be the peak for reservoirs like Brownlee and Paddock. If you've never tried crappie fishing, what are you waiting for? It's a whole lot of fun in small packages.

What To Use

Spinning Gear: The light spinning rod is the easiest rig to use for crappies. An ultra-light spinning reel and rod makes fishing for crappie even more fun because you can use four-pound-test line, which makes it easier to cast lightweight lures. The fish really put up a good fight on light gear.

Whatever kind of spinning gear you use, the lure of choice is the small jig. Jigs have changed over the years. The small, soft-plastic tube jig, which has a gummy feel to it, is the most popular type of lure. The bodies of the jigs are soft

and have a natural feel. Fish hit them quickly and hold on longer because of the natural feel.

I also like the feathered or small hair jigs but they're hard to find because they're outdated. Colors are important when it comes to crappie fishing. Good bets are pink and white, or red and white jigs. Popular colors change season after season.

A good way to fish a jig with a spinning rod is to attach a bobber to the line. You can adjust the depth of the jig by moving the bobber up and down. If the fish are hitting closer to the surface, say about three feet deep, then put the bobber 36 inches above the jig. If the fish are four feet deep or five feet deep, then move the bobber accordingly. Cast the rig out and let the bobber sit for a second. Then reel in a few feet and let it sit again. You should get a hit. If you really want to fish deep then just remove the bobber and let the jig sink to the bottom.

Don't forget spinners, like the Mepps. The No. 0 or 1 Aglia are great for crappies. Hot chartreuse with a squirrel tail is preferred by some fishermen. Mepps also puts out a Crappie Kit which has an assortment of small spinners and Mister Twister Curly Tails.

Fly Rod: Fly fishing for crappies is another fantastic way to catch them. Most fly fishermen use float tubes to go after the fish. You'll want to use a sinking fly line if the fish are deep. Take two reels in your float tube. One with sinking line and another with floating line. If the fish are close to the surface, you can switch to the reel with floating line.

The best flies for crappie are the Stayner Ducktail, Woolly Bugger, Fluff Butt or other small nymph fly patterns.

Cane Pole: You probably think I'm nuts, but a cane pole is a simple and great way to catch crappie. I once saw a guy using a cane pole and a jig along the bank at Paddock Reservoir. He would sneak along the bank and just dab the jig in the water about 6 or 7 feet off the bank. He had a gunny sack full of crappie. The cane pole is popular in the southeastern states and should be used here in Idaho, but they're pretty hard to find. Give it a try if you can find them, it's fun.

Where To Go

1. Brownlee Reservoir: This is probably the best crappie-fishing spot in Idaho, probably the West. The reservoir is 55 miles long and you'll have to locate the best areas. A boat gives you an advantage on this reservoir. Some of the key fishing spots are around Woodhead Park near the dam, which is east of Cambridge, or where the Powder River flows into the reservoir on the Oregon side.

Bank fishermen can do OK if they find the right cove or rocky point. You can fish the coves in a canoe, float tube or rowboat but be aware of the wind on this big reservoir.

The reservoir is accessible from I-84 from Ontario, Oregon, to Farewell Bend, the Old Ferry Road out of Weiser, or Highway 71 from Cambridge.

2. C.J. Strike Reservoir: This is another big reservoir (7,500 acres to be exact) where a boat is an advantage. You'll find crappies in the Bruneau River Arm of the reservoir and also in the Snake River Arm. A good spot in the past has been the Snake River Arm near Cove Arm Reservoir.

C.J. Strike Reservoir is located south of Mountain Home near the towns of Grand View and Bruneau.

3. Paddock Reservoir: This remote reservoir, located about 26 miles northeast of Payette, has long been a top crappie producer in southern Idaho. However, because of the drought, the reservoir was drained almost completely and the crappie population took a dive. It hasn't been the greatest fishing in recent years. Put this reservoir on your list for future years and hope the crappie populations make a comeback.

It is reached by driving Highway 52 between Emmett and Payette and taking Little Willow Creek Road.

4. Chain Lakes (north Idaho): If you've got a boat and want to do a little exploring, try the Chain Lakes off the Coeur d'Alene River. Some of them include Anderson Lake, Black Lake, Medicine Lake, Cave Lake, Rose Lake, and even the bays of Coeur d'Alene Lake.

Most anglers go after bass and northern pike in these lakes but there's no reason to forget the crappies. You can launch your boat at the boat ramp in downtown Coeur d'Alene and reach the lakes by going toward Harrison.

5. Salmon Falls Reservoir: This reservoir is located 9 miles west of Rogerson, which is south of Twin Falls. It has a fair population of crappies, but they're hard to find. The anglers who know the reservoir say fishing is best in the upper section in the gravel pit area. Sometimes you'll find the fish next to a piece of structure like a bush.

The reservoir is reached by driving U.S. 93 south of Twin Falls to Rogerson and turning west.

6. Smaller Reservoirs and Ponds: Crappie can also be found in Lake Lowell near Nampa, Crane Creek Reservoir, 35 miles northwest of Weiser, Horseshoe Bend Pond near Horseshoe Bend, Crane Falls Lake south of Mountain Home, Caldwell Ponds near Caldwell, and Sawyer Pond near Emmett.

Perch

If it's a lot of fish you want for the freezer, go after perch. Not glamorous enough like cutthroat trout or steelhead? Not a brute like the northern pike? Not mysterious, like the sturgeon? Well, when you fry up a pan full of fillets, you won't care. Taste is what it's all about.

Besides dinner, perch also give you hot action, that's if you find the schools at lakes and reservoirs like Cascade and C.J. Strike reservoirs and northern Idaho's Hayden Lake.

Here's another advantage of perch fishing. It's simple, so it's great for the kids. And your equipment doesn't have to be that elaborate. You can fish right off a dock or the bank with a bobber and a worm and catch as many as you like. Most perch you'll find in Idaho waters are about 7 to 9 inches long but some years reservoirs like Cascade will offer real whoppers going about 12 inches in length. I've caught perch through the ice, off the bank and even trolling for trout in a canoe. They're wild and can give you a good day of fishing.

What To Use

Still Fishing: The best way to catch perch is to start off with a two-hook rig and fish on the bottom. Use worms at first and after you catch the first perch, cut it up and use it for bait. That's where the term "cut bait" comes from. The best way to prepare perch for bait is to cut it up in strips and put it on the hook like sewing with a needle.

A good rig is the double hook set up. Go to the end of your line and about 24 inches up the line tie your first hook and leader. About 12 inches below that tie on another hook. At the end of the line put a small bell-shaped sinker. The best size hook is about No. 6.

You'll catch most of your perch on the bottom, although some anglers use a bobber and try to find at what depth in the reservoir perch are lurking. This can be effective when ice fishing.

You can also catch perch with a small jig, such as a red-and-white crappie jig. Most perch fishermen use spinning gear, but you can also catch them on a fly rod using small nymph patterns like Stayner Ducktails, Woolly Worms or Woolly Buggers.

Where To Go

1. Cascade Reservoir: Located about 74 miles north of Boise, this reservoir is one of the best for perch fishing in southern Idaho. Some of the best places around the reservoir are Poison Creek, Sugarloaf, Crown Point and along the area near the Cascade City Park.

You can get to the reservoir by driving State Highway 55 to the town of Cascade and going from there.

2. C.J. Strike Reservoir: Many areas of this reservoir, located between Grand View and Bruneau on the Snake and Bruneau rivers, have caches of perch. Fishing is good around the dam and particularly in the Narrows or by the C.J. Strike Wildlife Management Area.

3. Anderson Ranch Reservoir: This 5,000-acre reservoir is known for kokanee, trout and bass fishing, but a bank angler can also catch perch.

The reservoir is reached by driving east of Boise on I-84 and turning north on U.S. 20 at Mountain Home. Turn at the sign pointing to Anderson Ranch Dam for access to the reservoir. The shoreline around the upper end of the reservoir near Pine is also good for perch fishing.

4. Hayden Lake: This 4,000-acre lake can be reached by driving U.S. 95 north out of Coeur d'Alene about 4 miles and then going east 2 miles. It has trout, bass, crappie and whitefish but is known for perch fishing.

5. Carey Lake: This is a 200-acre lake located near the town of Carey. Take U.S. 20 north and east out of Mountain Home and continue toward Arco.

6. Bear Lake: Located on the Utah-Idaho border, this 120-square-mile lake has plenty of spots to go looking for perch. One of the major access points is east of the town of St. Charles off U.S. 89 at Bear Lake State Park or by taking the road that travels the east side of the lake.

7. Mud Lake: This lake is known for perch fishing, especially in the winter through the ice. It is reached by driving 4 miles east of Terreton on State Highway 28.

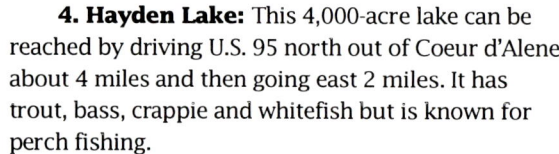

Woolly Bugger

Stayner Ducktail

Woolly Worm

Walleye

Drag a floating crankbait or spinnerbait across the shallow weed beds in Salmon Falls Creek Reservoir and you just might hook into a strange-looking fish. Idaho doesn't rate much when fishing magazines pick walleye hot spots. In fact, a lot of anglers in Idaho don't even know the state has walleye. Well, it does.

The toothy, wide-eyed fish can be found in Salmon Falls Creek Reservoir and Oneida Reservoir. Fishing's not hot and heavy. Chances are you'll have to work pretty hard for the fish.

Walleye were introduced in the state in 1974 and have done OK, not great, but OK. Water levels in the reservoirs fluctuate wildly and play havoc on fish spawning and nesting. Fish populations are maintained by stocking. When possible, millions of walleye fry are obtained from the Midwest and stocked in the reservoirs.

Most fish in Salmon Falls Creek Reservoir range from 5 to 10 pounds and from 18 to 30 inches. A 15.9 pound, 32 3/4-inch walleye was taken from the reservoir in 1987.

The best fishing in Idaho can be in March or early April when the fish are spawning. You'll find them on rocky shoals or in weed beds. Floating crankbaits or spinner baits work best during this time. In summer, when reservoir water warms up, walleye may go deep. Sometimes they are found in water as deep as 40 feet. Here, deep-diving crankbaits are a good bet.

Walleye also like to feed at night and can be found in the shallows after sundown.

What To Use

Gear - In Idaho you can get by with using your bass-fishing rods and reels. A medium-weight spinning rod and reel are good, too.

Lures - Bass lures are fine. You can take walleyes in the shallows with spinnerbaits or floating crankbaits, like Rapalas.

In other states, walleye fishermen can use live bait, such as minnows. That's not the case in Idaho, live minnows are illegal. So a good lure is a minnow-colored Rapala.

When perch are in deeper water, try a deep-diving crankbait like the Storm ThunderSticks or Deep Rattlin' Fat Rap. Lures such as the Timber Doodle or Mepps Black Fury Musky Killer can also be used for walleye.

A lot of anglers fish just off shore and cast toward the bank, retrieving the lure so it's going away from the shore. This can be deadly, especially for walleyes working shallow weed beds for minnows. If you're fishing in a little deeper water where the walleye may be suspended at a certain depth, you might try a lure like the Mepps Walleye Killer. The hook on the end of the lure can be baited with a dead minnow, some sucker meat, or a nightcrawler. The lure comes with blades in a variety of colors, such as silver, yellow, orange and brass.

Don't forget other typical bass lures, like jigs with plastic tails. Walleye have also been taken on spoons like large Dardevles.

Where To Go

1. Salmon Falls Creek Reservoir: This 3,520-acre reservoir is long and narrow and about 6 to 10 miles in length, depending on the amount of water being stored.

It is reached by driving south out of Twin Falls on U.S 93 as if you were heading for Jackpot, Nevada, to do a little gambling. In fact, you might just combine fishing and gambling. Once you reach Rogerson (still in Idaho), turn west and go 9 miles to the reservoir. If you can't find the walleye, Salmon Falls Creek Reservoir also has rainbow trout, crappie, kokanee and perch.

2. Oneida Reservoir: This 480-acre reservoir, located along the Bear River in southeastern Idaho, is also stocked with walleye. The reservoir can be reached by driving Idaho Highway 34 south of Grace. The reservoir is located between Grace and Preston, about 7 miles south of Thatcher.

Walleye Killer

Sturgeon

He's gonna surface. He's gonna surface. My heart leaped into my throat. I felt like Captain Ahab waiting for Moby Dick to come blasting out of the water. But I was on the Snake River, just below Swan Falls Dam, waiting to see my first white sturgeon come flying out of the river.

The 7-foot, 3 1/2-inch prehistoric creature flew out of the water like a missile being fired from a nuclear submarine. I was in awe just watching the fisherman rear back on the fishing rod and trying to keep the line taut. I had a ringside seat on the jet boat. The angler was sitting on a cooler in the back of the boat, braced for the upcoming battle. And what a battle it was. The estimated 200 pounds of fresh fish, twisting, turning and splashing in the river, was enough to make any mere mortal step back and take another look. I just hoped the 180-pound fisherman would stay in his seat and not go overboard.

"You wanna reel in some?" the crusty old angler said. I was a little scared I didn't want to blow the whole thing, but I decided to give it a try. It was like trying all the upper and lower body exercise machines at the local gym all at once. My arm, wrist, leg and back muscles were straining under the pressure. Sometimes it takes up to three anglers, taking turns during the hour-long battle, to finally get the fish in. I didn't last 15 minutes before giving up.

Until you actually feel a white sturgeon trying to rip the surf-fishing rod out of your hands, you don't realize why Idaho anglers spend all year long trying to hook into the giant toothless wonders.

Anglers in Idaho can catch sturgeon, but the fish have to be released unharmed. Rules are strict. You can't even take them out of the water. That's because dams and pollution on Idaho's rivers have taken their toll on the fish. Only about 4,000 of them remain in the Snake River. That's less than on the Kootenai River in northern Idaho. Only about 785 fish were in that river in September of 1994 when the U.S. Fish and Wildlife Service added the Kootenai River white sturgeon to the endangered species list.

You can still catch and release sturgeon in the Snake River. Anglers have to be careful and treat the fish properly, so fishing can continue. Fishing for sturgeon isn't just fishing. It's a fascination with a fish.

The sturgeon is a prehistoric critter that has evolved over the years and has been able to adapt, somewhat, to dams on the rivers. The fish needs free-flowing water to reproduce and has done so in certain stretches of the Snake River. Sturgeon have the dubious nickname of Vacuum Cleaner because they feed on the bottom and eat dead matter. They were once nominated for Idaho's state fish but someone in the Legislature called them a giant sucker. Needless to say, the honor went to the cutthroat trout.

Sturgeon can reach sizes up to 18 feet in length and weigh 1,385 pounds. But the largest fish found in recent times don't approach the sizes found in the late 1800s. In recent times, the oldest sturgeon aged by biologists in the Snake River was 65 years old and 11 feet long. The oldest checked in the Kootenai River was 46 years old and 8.3 feet long. An estimated 102-year-old fish was found in the Columbia River.

Sturgeon are fascinating, too, because pictures of them being dragged out of the water by old cars can be found in history books. Anglers wonder if the giants are still lurking in the waters of the Northwest. Idaho's rod and reel sturgeon record is 394 pounds. It was caught in the Snake River in 1956. The set line record is 675 pounds taken from the Snake River in 1908.

So you see, the more you learn about the fish, the more you want to go out and catch one.

What To Use

A smelt hooked on a 7/0 or 9/0 barbless hook is one of the best rigs. Use a rubber band to secure the smelt to the hook. Other types of fresh fish can also be used for bait. Anglers try to keep the bait on the bottom with big, 8-ounce sinkers.

Big catfish gear can be used, but serious sturgeon anglers use 12-foot surf-fishing rods with ocean-type reels. Your line has to be strong and 40- to 60-pound test is recommended.

Where To Go

The Snake River is a popular, and probably one of the only decent places, to fish for sturgeon in Idaho. Sections downstream from Bliss Dam (1.) to the backwaters of C.J. Strike Dam, and in Hells Canyon (3.) are the better sections to fish.

The Snake River below C.J. Strike Dam and Swan Falls Dam (2.) offers fair fishing. Sturgeon are also caught in the Lower Salmon River.

Fly Fishing for Steelhead

Plop! My first fly fishing experience on the Upper Salmon River for steelhead was anything but artistic. The fly hit the water like a cannonball. If there were any steelhead in the river, they high-tailed it for the deepest hole. Trying to cast a heavy fly rod, heavy line and a heavy fly had me up a creek. I looked like the worst student in a class of beginner fly casters, even though I had been fly fishing for trout for nearly 20 years.

But I didn't give up trying to cast the steelhead gear. I managed to get a cast off to a nice run in the middle of the river near North Fork, a place that becomes the steelhead-fishing capital of central Idaho. A couple of steelhead had already been taken along this stretch of the river that morning in March. Sun glistened off the 4-foot-high snowbanks on the sides of the river. The early spring day was pleasant, pleasant enough for me to go gloveless.

The tip of my rod vibrated as my fly bounced along the cobblestone bottom of the river. I had no idea what I was doing. Steelhead-fishing guide Jerry Meyers set me up with equipment and told me where to fish. Meyers runs Silver Cloud Expeditions, an outfitting service that specializes in fly fishing for steelies. Meyers is based in Salmon, Idaho.

The icy waters of the Salmon lapped against my neoprene chest waders as I watched the rod tip bounce. Suddenly, the line stopped. I was wondering what was going on, but Meyers knew right off the bat that a fish had grabbed my fly. Fish on! I was dazed. The fish made a V wake up the river. My reaction time was missing on all four cylinders. The steelie made a run and spit out the hook before I could set it. There I stood, sheepishly looking at Meyers. I had my chance at a spring steelhead and blew it.

I failed to hook that spring steelie, but you know, the experience had me hooked on fly fishing for these sea-run rainbows.

What To Use

- A pair of neoprene waders for wading the river.
- A 9 to 9 1/2-foot fly rod that will handle 7 to 9 weight line. The rod has to have the backbone to handle the fight of a steelhead.
- Floating line, a fast-sinking line, or 10- to 20-foot super-fast sink tip line.
- For a reel, you'll basically need a fly reel big enough to handle 100 to 150 feet of backing plus the fly line.
- Use a 7 1/2- to 9-foot leader with a 10- to 15-pound-test tippet.
- Here's a good selection of flies: Green-Butted Skunk, Purple Peril, Christmas Tree, Double Egg (orange and white or pink and white) and the Fall Favorite.

Where To Go

1. About 150 miles of the **Upper Salmon River** from North Fork (near Salmon) to Stanley offers good steelhead fishing in March and April. You can float the river in a drift boat or wade. The river's low enough so you can wade out on the gravel bars and get far enough from shore to get off a good cast.

Check with fishing shops in Stanley, Challis, Salmon or

North Fork for fishing conditions and what the fish are hitting.

2. The Salmon River around Riggins can be a good fly fishing stretch in both fall and spring, if the water's low. There are several gravel bars in the area that make for good wading, and fishing. This stretch is also conducive for fishing from a drift boat. Some of the best fly fishing is in mid-October when the steelhead run can be at its peak. The river is often at its lowest point and clear. In spring, the river in this area can be muddy and high.

Call outfitters or businesses in Riggins for details on this section.

3. The Clearwater River from Lewiston to Orofino is a good fly fishing stretch in both fall and spring, but it's mostly preferred in fall. Actually, the Clearwater River is one of the earliest places for fly fishing—September when the run is first starting.

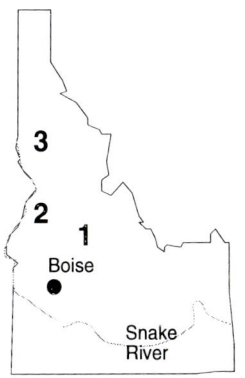

Fall Favorite

Purple Pevil

Green-Butt Skunk

Double Egg

Christmas Tree

Using Plugs for Steelhead

Rod tips vibrate. Oarlocks squeak and groan. Riffles in the Salmon River sound like a thousand uncapped bottles of bubbling tonic water. The rod tips are vibrating because deep-water steelhead lures are wiggling and bouncing off the river's cobblestone bottom.

Pulling plugs for steelhead is one of the most hypnotizing ways to fish. Sometimes I just forget about fishing as I row my battered and splintered drift boat back and forth across the river's pool and watch the vibration of the rods.

Orange and yellow leaves float by. The fall's wind chills my bones. Chukars badger me from the steep mountains above, daring me to chase them up the cliffs. But no shotguns today. I've got more important things to do, like stalking Idaho's magnificent steelhead. I've gone fishless many times back trolling, or Hot Shotting, for steelies, but it doesn't matter. It only takes the hit of one fish to make you keep coming back year in and year out.

I remember my first steelhead. I was fishing with McKay Bar Outfitters on the Salmon River a few miles downstream from the resort in the heart of the Frank Church River of No Return Wilderness.

I was a greenhorn on that fateful fall day in the late 1970s. I didn't know anything about bobbers and jigs, Sammies and shrimp, or Hot Shots. More than that, I didn't have a deep respect for the fish. I didn't realize steelhead had to swim 800 miles from the Pacific Ocean up the Columbia, Snake and Salmon rivers, dodging gill nets, dams, ocean fishermen and other anglers. Maybe that's the lure of the fish. The steelhead is one tough fish and deserves a lot of respect.

When I reeled in my first steelhead more than a decade and a half ago, it touched off something in me. I've been making the pilgrimage to steelhead waters every fall and spring. Sometimes I hook into them, sometimes I don't. But like I said, there's more to catching steelies than hooking fish—like being on the river.

What To Use

If you've got a drift boat or jet boat, Hot Shotting is one of the best methods. Steelhead fishermen take the fishing method of trolling and turn it backwards. That's right. The point of back trolling is to keep the boat still in the river and let the current work the lure. When the fishing line is held taut, the river current pushes against the crankbait, making it wiggle and dive to the bottom of the river.

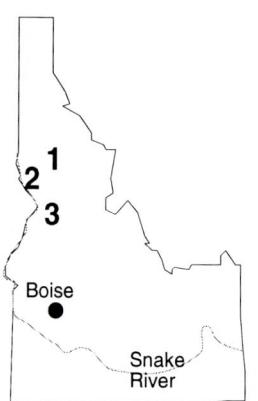

Unlike regular trout, which stay at the head of the river's pools, steelhead favor the bottom part of the pool, or the tailout. They come through the rapids of a river and then rest. Drift boaters and jet boaters sweep their boats back and forth across the river taking their plugs across the tailout of the pool.

They slowly work their way downstream from the middle of the pool to the end of the pool. Usually at the edge of the tailout, just upstream from the rapids, is where the steelhead are lying.

Some of the best lures for Hot Shotting are Hot Shots, of course, Hot 'N Tots, and Wiggle Warts. I've also hooked steelhead on large Flatfish.

Clearwater steelhead fishermen have perfected another sure-fire method—the bobber and jig. The bobber and jig works especially well in low water.

A Sammie and shrimp, used to drift through river holes, is another proven method. A Sammie or other drift lure, such as the Li'l Corky, is used with shrimp or fresh roe. Steelhead fishermen switch from plugs to drifters and bait as water temperatures drop.

Pulling plugs and using bobbers and jigs work best in October, but anglers usually switch to drifters and bait in November.

Where To Go

1. Clearwater River: Steelhead usually start showing up in the lower Clearwater River at the confluence of the Snake River in September. It's usually the earliest steelhead fishing in Idaho. The Clearwater from Lewiston to Orofino can offer some of the best fishing in September, but it's catch-and-release until mid-October. From that time through March is a good time to fish the river.

2. Snake River: The river from Lewiston to Hells Canyon Dam is good for fishing in fall. Hot spots are at Lewiston, Asotin, Washington, at the confluence of the Salmon River where fish bunch up, and at Hells Canyon Dam.

3. Salmon River: The whole river, from the confluence of the Snake to Challis can offer good steelhead fishing.

Northerns

There's a flash. You heart misses a beat. The Johnson Silver Minnow skims across a shallow underwater cabbage patch in northern Idaho's Blue Lake. Could there be a 10- to 20-pound notorious northern pike lurking nearby?

Within seconds the graphite bait-casting rod bends under the pressure of a thrashing northern. The drag buzzes and excitement builds as my fishing partner and I wait for a good look at the fish. But this time it's disappointment. The fish is only about 16 inches long. It's a mere baby up here and not even worth mentioning at the local fishing shop. You'd be laughed out of the local bar.

But most anglers don't give up. Throughout spring, summer and fall, anglers in northern Idaho go from dawn to dusk searching for trophy northern pike—the ones over 30 pounds. That's what we're talking about up here—trophy fish. Northerns bigger than some of those you'd catch in Canada.

C'mon, northern pike? Yup. They're up here. The typical reaction, when you tell someone that these strange-looking Midwest imports are really lurking in northern Idaho's beautiful lakes, is disbelief. Northerns are not native to Idaho. These razor-tooth, duck-mouth fish can best be described as Idaho's answer for a swimming Mack truck.

Once feared as the godzilla that would take over Idaho and annihilate every fish in its path, the northern pike is now a revered game fish.

Pike were illegally stocked in Cave and Medicine lakes in northern Idaho in 1972 or 1974. The Idaho Department of Fish and Game believed the so-called "wash-tub" style plants included about a dozen fish from Lone Pine Reservoir in Montana. In the early 1970s rumors floated around the Osburn-Kellogg area that northerns had been illegally stocked in the lakes, but the talk never resulted in anything until someone brought an 8-pound pike into a Fish and Game office in 1975.

Today pike inhabit the Chain lakes along the Coeur d'Alene River and throughout the bays of Coeur d' Alene Lake. They're also in the St. Joe, Pend Oreille, and Priest river systems, and some lakes near the Washington state border.

Pike are voracious eaters and very prolific. Their long lean bodies, huge teeth and big mouths make them eating machines that will take anything from fish to frogs to snakes and ducklings—even muskrats. I wonder if I can find a lure that represents a muskrat? At any rate, I'll be back up north some day looking for that trophy northern pike.

What To Use

Use a heavy-duty, bait-casting or spinning outfit, the kind you use for bass fishing. Line should be 10- to 20-pound test.

For lures, try the Johnson Silver Minnow or other silver or

gold weedless spoons, in sizes 1/4 to 1/2 ounce, are best for the shallow, weedy areas. Put a pork skirt on to add extra color. A ripple rind in a red or yellow is recommended.

Dardevles in 3/4 to 1 ounce are a good bet for deeper water. The best colors are red and white, black and white or the Five of Diamond style.

Spinnerbaits are good for working shallow weed patches. White, chartreuse and orange are the color choices of local anglers. Fishermen mix and match skirts and blades in different colors.

A bucktail spinner, such as a Mepps Giant Killer, can be the ticket in both shallow and deep water. Try it in orange, red or yellow.

Plugs, such as the big jointed Rapalas or Zara Spooks are well known pike lures.

Bait, such as smelt, are used for winter fishing through the ice.

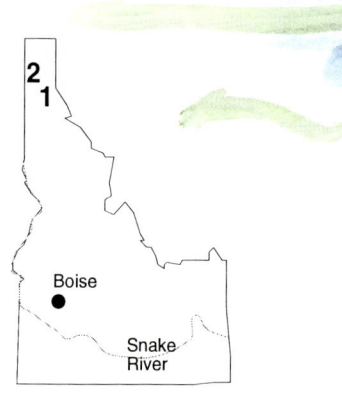

Seasons

Spring: Avid pike fishermen hit the shallow weedy areas in the chain lakes or on the inside of the bays of Coeur d'Alene Lake. Look for underwater patches of cabbage or salad grass. As a general rule, you'll catch bass and pike in the same weed beds. Bass mostly stay on the inside of the weed beds while pike are on the outside.

Summer and Fall: Pike move into deeper water, around 12 to 14 feet deep, with lots of under cabbage. This is number 1 pike water. It can be found in the Chain lakes or the bays of Coeur d'Alene Lake.

Winter: Late-season ice fishing is best in the area lakes when pike are cruising in the pre-spawning state.

Where To Go

Try any one of the Chain lakes (1.), such as Killarney, Thompson, Cave, Swan, Rose, Blue, Black or Anderson lakes, located along the Coeur d'Alene River above Coeur d'Alene Lake (2.). In Coeur d'Alene Lake, hit the bays on the north end. Cougar Bay seems to be a good spot at times.

Mackinaw

Payette Lake looks almost silver in the mid-morning light. Canada geese float on the air currents above the lake as they cruise the shoreline in an every-day spring ritual. A few mergansers swim along the bank with their heads bobbing underwater for anything they can catch for breakfast. It's May and snow caps the mountains around McCall like icing on a forested cake.

A boat cruises about 100 yards off shore, barely making a wake. Two fishermen are huddled inside, dressed in rain gear and winter clothing. They stare at their lines dragging from both sides of the boat.

Hour upon hour floats by. They cruise and wait. They're waiting for the hit of a lake trout. Lake trout, or mackinaw as they are called by locals, are some of Idaho's largest trout, ranging in size from 10 to 57 pounds. They're difficult to catch and a fisherman may go days or even years without catching one. But it only takes one on the line to start a life-long passion.

Spring is a good time to fish for mackinaw because they come out of the depths of the lake and cruise the shallows in search of food after being under the ice all winter. It's a time when you'll see a lot of boats on Payette Lake patrolling the shorelines in search of the fish. Spring is a time of year when the water temperature is pretty uniform throughout the whole lake and you can catch the fish on shallow gear. You don't need down riggers like other times of the year when the surface gets warm and fish go deep.

Lake trout fishermen belong to a fraternity of sorts. They are initiated by that first hit of a lake trout and then they are sworn to a code of silence. Just try and talk to one about what they are using for fishing, and you won't get a straight answer. "Oh, Bob's lure is best." "Well, what the heck is Bob's lure." "Can't tell you." You can't blame them. Lake trout fishing is tough and the less competition the better.

Lake trout were introduced in Idaho and can be found in several lakes from the northern Panhandle to the Utah border.

What To Use

Gear: Use a heavy-duty spinning or bait-casting rod and reel.

Flatfish: You can't go wrong with a Flatfish but make sure it's big enough. You'll see fishermen using 4- to 5-inch Flatfish in a variety of colors. The best colors are orange or fluorescent red, frog, coho-silver, perch and rainbow.

Other Plugs: Other deep-diving crankbaits, such as large perch-colored Rapalas will get down for lake trout.

Spoons: Big red and White Dardevle or steelhead spoons are a good bet. Krocodile lures also work.

Spinners: Try an orange Mepps Giant Killer. Lake trout feed on kokanee, which turn orange when they are spawning.

Bait: Lake trout like freshwater shrimp. A good bet would be deep-running pop gear, such as a Ford Fender, followed by a Wedding Ring spinner topped off with bait shrimp.

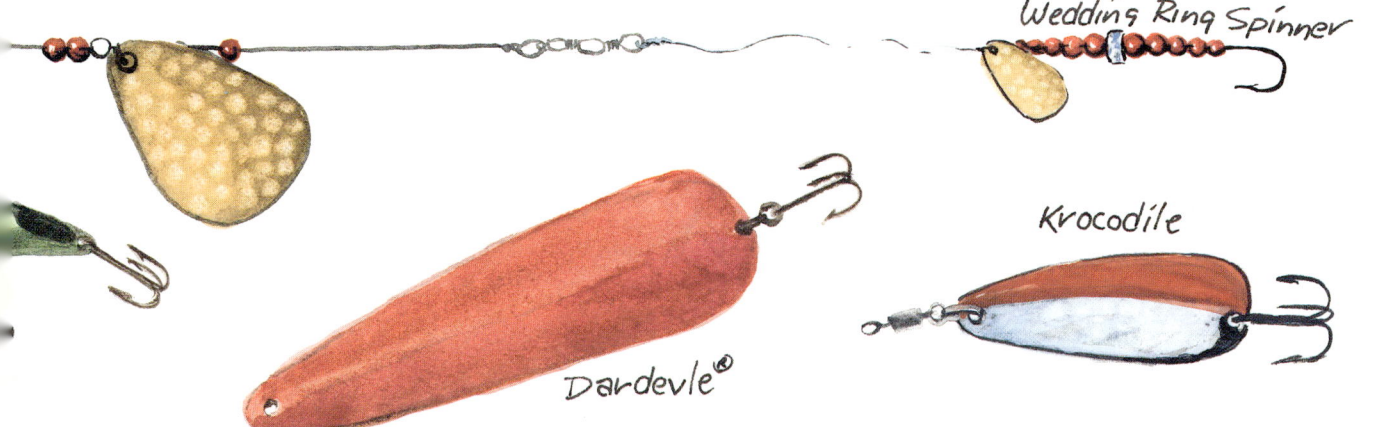

Wedding Ring Spinner

Dardevle®

Krocodile

Where To Go

1. Priest Lake: This is probably one of Idaho's best known lakes for lake trout. This is where anglers have taken lake trout over 50 pounds. There are two Priest lakes, the upper one and the main lake. The main lake is 19 miles long. On the way to the lake you'll find resorts, tackle shops and campgrounds. So ask around and find out what the macks are hitting.

Take U.S. 2 west from Sandpoint to Priest River. Head north on Highway 57 and follow the signs to the lake.

2. Pend Oreille Lake: Located right at Sandpoint, this huge 80,000-acre lake also has lake trout. There are plenty of fishing and boating shops in the area to get the lowdown on where to find lake trout.

3. Payette Lake: Located right at the town of McCall, this 1,000-acre lake is easily accessible from the Sports Marina in town, North Beach State Park or Ponderosa State Park. The best thing to do at this lake is to watch where other anglers are trolling and do the same.

4. Warm Lake: Located about 25 miles east of Cascade on the Warm Lake Highway. This lake is pretty small for mackinaw fishing, only being about 640 acres. But maybe that means less area to explore and look for fish. Late spring is definitely the best time for mackinaw fishing here.

5. Stanley Lake: Located about 8 miles west of Stanley, not many people know this lake has mackinaws. But every spring you hear of a few 10 pounders being caught. One nice thing about it, the lake is very scenic for fishing because it's located on the edge of the Sawtooths.

6. Bear Lake: There's plenty of room for exploring on this lake, which spans 120 square miles. It too is known for its lake trout. The lake is located on the Utah-Idaho border. It is reached by taking U.S. 89 south of Montpelier. Some of the best fishing is located on the east side of the lake in early spring.

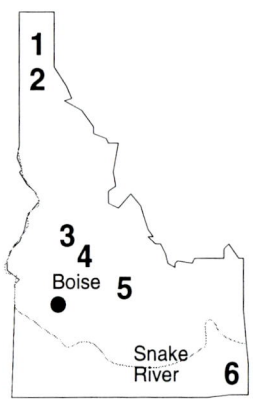

Catch and Release

Some folks love to fish but don't like to eat fish. They're real conservationists. They just enjoy the fun of catching fish and then releasing them. Other folks look forward to cooking up a day's catch and would like to have it no other way. Well, you can have it both ways in Idaho. There are plenty of fish to eat and plenty of fish that should be released to preserve fishing.

Idaho annually stocks more than 2.5 million fish in its lakes and streams that range in size from 8 to 10 inches. They are basically put in waters so anglers can take them out. Hence, the nickname for the program, called "put and take" trout fishing. It's no sin to keep trout that are stocked in streams and lakes. That's what they are there for. For the stocking program to be cost effective, the trout that are released in the state's waters have to be caught by anglers. If the trout just end up being washed away or dying, it's a waste of time and money.

Fish and Game gives out information on where trout are stocked, whether it's the Boise River through downtown Boise, Horsethief Reservoir in Valley County, or Day Rock Pond in Shoshone County. The state agency concentrates its stocking program in areas where anglers will get them. So, go out and get them and fry them up if you want.

Then there are the wild trout streams. These are areas where fish should be released to preserve the wild strains of fish. An example is the Middle Fork of the Salmon River where wild cutthroats live. An example of put-and-take is the Middle Fork of the Payette River where fishing is only as good as the number of trout that are stocked.

If you really want to fill your freezer with fish fillets for the winter, you should concentrate on warm-water fish, such as perch, bluegills, crappie and catfish. These fish are usually plentiful and catching a hundred or so for the freezer doesn't usually put a dent in the fish populations. We're lucky in Idaho to have fish like this. That way we can have our cake and eat it too. You can have fish for eating and wild fish for a variety of catching.

Back in the '60s, when I first started fly fishing in Idaho, I remember the trout limit was 15 fish. Wow, can you imagine catching 15 trout and actually being able to take them home? What's even more incredible is that on some of those cutthroat streams you could catch your limit of 15 trout in about an hour.

Today, the same streams have a slot limit where you can't take any cutthroat between 8 and 16 inches. You're lucky if you even catch one or two cuts in that range in a day's fishing. It's sad, but we will probably never take cutthroats home for the frying pan like we used to. But there are other kinds of fish for the pan.

Some trout and bass and wild steelhead have to be released so that Idaho's wild strains will live on. To allow us to have a variety of fishing, there's always put-and-take trout fishing or perch, crappie or bluegill fishing. OK, how do you release a fish so it can live for another day?

Here are tips from Idaho Fish and Game:
- Use artificial flies and lures and a single, barbless hook.
- Don't play the wild fish so that it gets tired out and can't recover.
- Don't squeeze the fish.
- Don't touch the gills or hold the fish by the gill covers.
- Leave the fish in the water while removing the hook. Needlenose pliers or forceps are a big help.
- If the hook cannot be easily removed, cut the leader. The hook will rust out.
- If the fish is exhausted, hold it in a swimming position in the water and move it back and forth gently until you release it.
- Avoid excessive and unnecessary handling of the fish. Avoid removing it from the water.

A lot of anglers want to take a picture of a big fish and hold it up out of the water before releasing it. This does more harm than good. It might be well worth it to forget the picture.

Catch and keep what fish are best for the frying pan and let the wild ones go. Good fishing.

About the Author and Artist

Pete Zimowsky

Pete Zimowsky is at home on the stream with his favorite fly rod. He has been roaming the streams and lakes of Idaho for more than 30 years. He has learned a lot about fishing in his 21 years as outdoor writer with the Idaho *Statesman* in Boise. He and his wife, Jan, live in Boise, Idaho. They have three children, James, Christine and Andy.

Patrick Davis

Patrick Davis is an illustrator and senior graphic artist for the Idaho *Statesman*. He lives in Boise with his wife, Virginia, and two sons, Todd and Mason.